THE ECONOMIC PINCH

LINDBERGH

The ECONOMIC PINCH

BY

C. A. LINDBERGH

THE NOONTIDE PRESS

THE NOONTIDE PRESS
1822 1/2 Newport Blvd. Suite #183
Costa Mesa, CA 92627

FIRST PUBLISHED, 1923
REPRINTED 1968, 1989

ISBN 0-939482-15-0

MANUFACTURED IN THE UNITED STATES OF AMERICA

CONTENTS

I	A Key to the Good Things	9
II	Three Useful Groups; One Useless Group	17
III	The American Nobility	21
IV	The Capital and Labor Conflict ..	25
V	The Capitalistic Aim	36
VI	Classification of Property Relations	45
VII	The Press, and Others	54
VIII	Believing + Voting — Thinking..	66
IX	Banks and the People	77
X	The Federal Reserve Act	83
XI	Panics Now Scientifically Created	94
XII	The War Boom	99
XIII	War Deflation	103
XIV	Ultimate Breakdown, or Radical Change	108
XV	The Esch-Cummins Railway Act.	120

CONTENTS

XVI "Congressional Investigations".. 124
XVII The Rules of Congress 133
XVIII The Legislative Bloc 143
XIX From Lowest to Highest 150
XX Economic Evil, and "Progressives" 169
XXI Government; Nation; People 181
XXII The Way Out 191

BOOK II

I The Greatest Game 199
II Team-Work for Victory 210
III The American Federations 217
IV World Relations 221
V By the People—For the People.. 236
General Index 247

THE ECONOMIC PINCH

BOOK I

THE ECONOMIC PINCH

I

A KEY TO THE GOOD THINGS

There's a key to the good things of the world. We all have the key. That key is the mind. It is *thought* that opens the way to all things.

It is our failure to give a little honest thought to direct our actions that compels most of us to struggle with the hardships of the world. We are too much under the influence of others —just a few—some of whom we are taught to worship, while still others whom we seldom even know control the things that control us.

As soon as we free ourselves from the domination of leaders—stop worshiping the self-appointed directors of our affairs, and instead look to the cause of things and have a mind on what action should be taken, just so soon shall we be freed from the fetters that now bind us to trouble. Then and then only infinite good as well as prosperity shall belong to all of us.

To waste our time in praising a few persons who pretend they do so much, but do nothing, on the other hand belittling other people because they have not done enough for us, is an admission of our own failure.

It is time that the people who do the useful things stand out in the world for positive action in their own common interest, instead of longer allowing themselves to become the victims of false leadership.

If we were to walk over a farmer's premises and let the farmer be our guide, he would tell us about his crops, his stock, his buildings and his other farm things. He could tell us of bad luck—that his work is all a gamble—that the weather, the prices that he gets if he produces something to sell, the price he has to pay for what he buys, are none of them controlled by him. His story would be truth, but he toils on through the years in spite of adverse facts. He varies his work a little from year to year, but whatever he gets is measured out to him by the same process. He never knows in advance what will happen to him. His work and his life are a gamble.

If we follow a workman into a shop or to his work whatever it may be, and let him explain his condition and the things that surround and happen to him, he too has a hard luck tale. He has his troubles. His pay may be fixed so that neither sunshine, rain nor drought will strike him directly, but he does not know when his job will end nor what he can buy with his wages. He seldom fixes the wages, and the price of what he must purchase is also always fixed for him, by others. He must work, without assurance, for the future. His future too is a gamble. The years roll on and he "sticks." He is forced to stick, as long as he is allowed to. He decides nothing that controls him.

Go with a so-called business proprietor into his store or other place of business, let him be the spokesman for what the world does to him.

He too it appears has his troubles. It is shown that most small business proprietors fail in time. When they fail they are worse off than even the farmer and the wage worker. They are left with a bankrupt past, while a penniless future stares them in the face. They are mostly unfitted to farm even if they had farms, and are at a disadvantage as wage workers. Their past is lost, and their future a gamble.

We have checked off three groups: the farmer, the wage worker and the so-called business man. Each looks with a certain amount of envy upon the other. The farmer sees the shorter hours of the city worker, his fixed wages, and usually notes with envy the latter's abode in the city; the wage worker sees the farmer as his own boss, running his farm, living in the pure country air, free of the foul smells of city garbage, sewers and much offal. Both look with envy on the business proprietor, thinking he has it easier; while the last is wondering how he can ever manage a change to something else.

But there is a fourth group, the profiteers of peace, the patrioteers of war, who busy themselves with the other three groups, exploiting them. Some of them do useful work in addition to their profiteering. Originally they were much like the rest of us. Most of them were born from our ranks—simply the more persevering and cunning, who have seen the hopelessness of our neglect of the big things that control the world. So they have taken possession, running all things to suit themselves.

We have the four groups to deal with, and the question is, what shall be done? That is the problem we shall consider. It is not our object here to discuss law nor attempt to point out specific remedies for prevailing wrongs. The purpose is to prove the necessity for a people's forum free from political prejudice, to pass on what is wrong in our laws and practices, to suggest correctives.

Incident to the discussion it is necessary to present a few fundamental principles involved in such a discussion. By way of explanation some laws and practices are referred to. There are many laws that operate against our reasonable independence, but none go so far in that direction as our finance and transportation laws, with the practices under them. They will be referred to because of that fact. Many old laws must be repealed, others amended and new codes of action provided for the regulation of business before we can become independent.

Politics are ancient and seem to have been the first plan for some sort of organization to give the people an expression en masse.

Politics were crude originally, and while they are extremely adroit now, they still fail to give the public much in the way of satisfaction. The object of the public, in political action, is to better conditions, and the object of most politicians is to hold office. To say the least it is a slow way to correct the errors that creep into affairs of mankind. It works something like the laws of evolution—so slowly that the ones who sow seldom live long enough to be in at the harvest.

Nearly every political move so far, when intended for the benefit of all the people, has failed because there was no sufficiently definite businss plan on which to act. Even when elections have been won in whole or in part, before the leaders could secure results they became tired, gave up, went over to the other side, and voters stood betrayed. The exceptions are few. The failure to progress in politics is due to the fact that politics *alone* are depended on by the public to correct errors in our public and business organization.

Usually it takes several campaigns to win an election for any progressive cause. The voters become dissatisfied with the old ways and finally they vote in protest, instead of having a definite plan for action when they win. Anything they consider is likely to be at least as good as the old, so they take a chance.

There are always candidates with rosy promises who wedge into such moves. They present themselves as the new "Moses," but all they know is to criticise the old—a thing that any one can simply do. These would-be saviors are beginners—they see the wrong but not the remedy, and in spite of their best intentions, the cause is lost before they start, even if they win an election. They are governed by the laws and conditions in force, and are not prepared to put into action anything progressive. The very fact that changes are proposed makes enemies of those who already have what they want, so they buck against anything new.

The laws favor the old political and profiteer groups; they made the laws. The groups hold up business—making people doubtful about what will happen if changes are made. "The time is not quite ripe"—"they view with alarm." To scare the people still more the old forces predict even positive calamity, if improvements are proposed. Often calamity does result from the mere suggestion, because business is timid and stops to see what will happen. Then the people who fought for reform no longer help; men and things return to the old way.

History tells of various political moves, through many ages, to correct evils taken as a first and only step. Several have occurred in our generation, but nothing has been gained for industrial independence.

We have always gone backward. Failure is due to the fact that we do not understand our business interests as they relate to each other. We cannot agree politically unless our business interests bring us together. For that reason our business interests should first be considered.

II

THREE USEFUL GROUPS; ONE USELESS GROUP

We economically divide ourselves into three useful groups: the farmer for agriculture; the wage workers for other industries; and the business group, with the help of the others, to manage exchange and distribution. Business men are not ordinarily called workers; neither are the farmers and wage workers termed business men, but all are workers and all do business.

The three groups are necessary. They have interests in common, but to their own misfortune they have been at least half antagonistic to each other, especially politically. All three have been the losers by that fact. As a matter of fact, not one can succeed without the others. Not one can be as prosperous with either of the others not prosperous, as when all are prosperous. The fourth group blocks the way to real prosperity of the other three. It always has—

but it shall not always. This fourth group I do not class with the useful, though to some extent some of those in it do more or less useful work.

The profiteers use judgment in their management. They first agree on how business should be arranged to give them the advantage of the other three groups, and then they adjust politics to that purpose. By subterfuge they successfully split up the other three partly unorganized groups, and manage to "capture" enough of their leaders out of the several organizations to control legislation and administration.

The useful groups—even in their most successful periods—have never secured that degree of prosperity which their services justify, because at all times they were and are exploited by the fourth group. The three useful groups have no central organization that includes them all, wherein to iron out their differences. They have simply group organizations, and these too often conflict with each other in their purposes.

A three-group *federation organization* could be formed so as not to interfere with any existing, useful single-group organizations. On the contrary, it would help them all by establishing a common field in which they could group their conference committees for the adjustment of respective rights. That done, they could go before any official body with rights presented and supported by all three useful groups. When they shall do that and present their demands in concrete form, it would not matter much who the public officials were, or what political party was in power—officials would be forced to act on the united interests of united demands, and they would have no way to dodge.

The United States Chamber of Commerce (a wholly private and not a governmental organization) was organized on behalf of the fourth group. The profiteers function politically through that organization, the business plans are first formed and then politics are controlled accordingly. The United States Chamber of Commerce does not present to Congress and other public American bodies polite requests that the public officials pass new laws, or take some action, without defining just what the laws to be passed are or what specifically shall be done. The bills and proposed acts are drafted and presented by someone representing interests supported by the Chamber of Commerce, all in form to be acted on; and the demand made that they be acted upon exactly as presented. The thing proposed is first put in concrete form and then goes through substantially the very way the profiteers decree.

Not only do the fourth group draft their own bills, but since the people—when they do make a feeble demand for a new law—ask simply that a law be passed or somehow get their demand in a party platform, the fourth group even draft the bill for that. They give it a title that promises what the useful groups want, but the body of the bill takes from them what the title promises, and frequently actually makes things worse than if left without action.

Something practical must be done to protect the country from its present situation. Existing economic conditions are intolerable; the laws and practices that govern business and politics are leading on to chaos. Action must be taken to save this nation from an impending peril.

III

THE AMERICAN NOBILITY

We can turn back the pages of history—to the kings of Europe, for instance. The kings were not strong enough to force the nobility to pay their share of the taxes and bear their part of the burdens, so the taxes and burdens were levied against the peasants. That gave revolutions—our own, for example. In this country now, the profiteers forming the fourth group, may be said to ape the old European nobility, but they have better fortified themselves. They also refuse to pay their share of taxes and bear their share of burdens, so the taxes and burdens are mostly shifted onto the useful groups—who bear them. It is time to take heed of conditions, lest disaster overtake us.

The profiteers are selfishly successful because they live by exploiting the rest of us. So we are hard up; and no really useful occupational group, acting separately, can make progress against the profiteers' exploitations. The useful groups must be active in their several ways, but first they must have a common field in which they can cooperate for common welfare. They should not be pulling in different directions if they are to get out of the political and business chaos that now confronts the world.

Shortly after the Civil War a group of men formed a selfish plan to rule the world by the manipulation of finances. Through money control they organized trusts to control transportation and the most important channels of distribution. With the control of finances and transportation they easily formed the other trusts.

They succeeded in all they designed, even to the rule of the majority of public officials, State and National. Land grants, mineral grants, timber grants, water-powers and other gifts and favors at the hands of Congress and state legislatures came practically for the asking.

The profiteers now fix the prices on what they buy from the people and on what they sell to the people. Because the profiteers have trusts, the plain people are forced to sell and buy mostly through the trusts. The profiteers are criminally indifferent to the rights of everybody outside their own group. They rob the people by authority of law. Public officials subservient to the trusts have made the laws to suit the trusts. The people have tried to get political action to release them from their bondage, but whichever party they have voted into power, its officials have betrayed the people. Exceptions have been few; never enough at any one time to be effective in giving relief from the existing and oppressive laws.

Because of the selfish, wholesale control of the world's different agencies for serving the necessities of ordinary mankind, and the failure of public officials to do their duty, many have become discouraged and given up all hope of relief from what is becoming intolerable.

The industrial and business confusion, and the political fiascoes have made numerous interests even more indifferent to the rights of mankind and created contempt for the law. Already the nation is shocked by what may be termed an epidemic of crime, constantly on the increase. Many in high places, instead of seeking to remedy the cause, are seeking to deal out greater punishment to the wrongdoers, most of whom are industrial and law-made criminals. We have almost reached a state of anarchy as a result of these conditions.

The strangest of all, in this world's confusion, is the fact that the profiteers with all their business shrewdness are forging ever on in their mad swoop to grab all the world's wealth—stranger still that their experts, of which they have thousands, do not understand that their clients are now driving to destruction with terrific speed. So far as surface appearances go there is but one hope for them—not that they will save themselves—but that the people will take action to save the people from the impending peril of the super-wealthy gone wealth crazy. And in the struggle of the people to save themselves those profiteers may be saved—not as profiteers, but from their own wild race for stolen wealth.

IV

THE CAPITAL AND LABOR CONFLICT

The administration of government and the transaction of business have created conflict between capital and labor. That conflict harms the farmer; it harms the wage worker; it harms all the useful in business. If it continues much longer to follow the present lead it will wreck all of us, the capitalist included. At present, however, the capitalist has the best of it.

If we were to start anew with an example similar to our own, of some other people, to judge from, we would not follow our present plans. We would map out quite a different course, politically as well as industrially. We cannot start on an entirely new political plan and even the business plan must be gradually modified in order to prevent chaos. We must follow our existing legal ways to modify things, to make them what they should be.

It is the crushing domination of property

interests over human rights that makes trouble. The working people do not deny the right of everybody to own property, but all who work for a living do deny the right of the owners to use property as a means to subject the industry of men, women and children to a toll creating industrial slaves of us. Nevertheless, the law is against us. The law permits, and in some cases directs, a measure of profit in favor of property interests which, if followed only another generation, would be completely disastrous. It means ultimate destruction of the nation unless the people take unto themselves the initiative to enforce the rights guaranteed by the fundamental laws of nature, and by the Constitution itself in the spirit and the letter of its makers.

Congress by numerous acts, the Interstate Commerce Commission and other public bodies by their acts, and the courts by their decrees,—have all enforced rules that operate against the people who are forced to work for a living, and against business itself with special-privilege exemptions. The specially privileged have constantly been given greater and greater power, until now the wealthy are firmly saddled and spurred on the backs of the people.

The wealth of the country should be an asset and not a liability to its workers. But the rules that govern us now make centralized wealth a very heavy liability. Under present conditions the more we produce on the farm and from wage work to sell or furnish to the trusts at low cost to them—for the trusts to resell to consumers at enormous profit, further centralizing capital—the more we are charged to pay dividends, interest and rents on their increasing capital.

Those who now control seek to sidetrack discussion of this by bringing up other subjects. They wish to divert our thoughts to mixed farming, increased production, cooperative buying and selling, and a lot of other subjects and dodge a discussion of the blighting of humanity by excessive charges for the use of capital.

Farmers and others will realize more keenly how centralized wealth has become a liability to us, instead of an asset, by considering an incident that followed close after the World War.

During the war the profiteers inflated everything. They ran prices up so rapidly that in the comparatively short period many thousand new millionaires were made, and most of those who were millionaires before added tens and hundreds of millions to their dollar pile. Of course, the farmer and wage worker and common business interests got in somewhat on the high prices, but they got only a nibble, and most of what they got—in some cases all of it and still more—has already been taken from them by the trick of deflation.

The millions of wealth of the millionaires—tens of billions in the aggregate, made out of the war inflation—wouldn't count to its greatest power if that accumulated wealth had to pay full value for farm products, and then again to the wage workers. Something would have to be done, these profiteers concluded, to force the price of farm products down, and in addition deflate wages. For it is a fact that no capital, however great, can accumulate to equal the earnings of the workers. If the workers had any way at all of conserving the products of their energy for themselves, there would be no conflict between capital and labor. It is because of capital's taking an unreasonable toll that conflict results.

After the war, but while inflation was still on, the war millionaires, cooperating with certain high government officials, spread propaganda among the farmers to increase farm production, because the world—Europe especially—was starving and the American farmer should be loyal to humanity, and increase his crops. Those profiteers and their allied public officials shouted that if the farmer would thus save the world from starvation, in addition to doing that noble act he would also reap great profit.

The patriotic farmer, in response to the call from public officials and the profiteer-inspired press, and believing in the spirit of this world call, bought extra machinery, went to additional expense in various ways, worked himself and his family harder to increase the farm product. To his disappointment, when the crop was produced the farmer found that the Federal Reserve Board had just in advance of his marketing the crops, put on deflation. The farmer, owing to the high price of machinery and other costs, as based on former inflation, was now compelled to sell his crop below cost. Meantime the wage worker was deflated by forced idleness and reduced wages.

If the farmer could have taken his loss and been done with it, he might still have hoped, but our economic system would not permit the farmer to end his trouble even there. The profiteer bought his crop at less than it cost to produce and resold it at enormous profit, adding that profit to his already swollen wealth. Upon this added wealth both the farmer and the deflated wage worker, and their children after them, must all their days pay additional rent, dividends and interest; since the profiteer took his wealth to buy from the impoverished farmers and other workers their Liberty Bonds and other valuable property at great discount. All this is now controlled by centralized wealth, used as a basis to be charged against the producing energy of all who work to live.

The additional rake-off of the capitalists, secured through the tricks of inflation and deflation, has become vested capital on which farmers and others will have to pay additional rents, dividends and interest—computed by the rules fixed by law in some cases, with still larger profit allowed by practice in others. It will go on compounding as the years roll by until we can no longer work long enough nor hard enough to pay it. That is what is meant by saying that centralized capital has become a liability, and is not an asset as it should be.

The capitalist is given a legal guarantee of profit while the worker has no guarantee. On the contrary, the worker is forced to earn the profit for the capitalist, but never a word to compare that with a reasonable wage to the wage worker nor reasonable pay to the farmer for the farm product.* Capital is always uppermost in the eye of the public officials. If a

*Attacking the theory of "the living wage" as a basis for determining the wages of railroad workers, the United States Railroad Labor Board in an opinion made public October 29, 1922, declared that such a course "if carried to its legitimate conclusion, would wreck every railroad in the United States, and if extended to other industries, would carry them into communistic ruin. . . . but the abstract, elusive thing called the living wage, confessedly based upon a makeshift and a guess, cannot receive the sanction of this Board, because it would be utterly impractical and would not be 'just and reasonable' as the law demands."

hint is given to the contrary, capital goes on a strike. When capital goes on a strike the public press does not call it a strike. It calls it hard times, or a panic, and lays no blame to capital. When the wage worker goes on a strike he is condemned by the capitalist, the press generally supports the capitalist, and often military forces are called to interfere with the striker, but never to interfere with the capitalist whatever his operations may be.

No strike of the wage worker that ever took place passed on to the public anything equal to the loss caused by the capitalists' strike of the last three years. The wage workers' strike has been practically forced by the capitalists' 1920-1922 financial strike. The farmer has no practical way to strike even if he could afford to. No more the small business man.

The Railway Labor Board and the public and private occurrences relating to the railway strike, furnish an example in point on a measure between capital and labor. In its decision on wages, and rules to govern the workers the Railway Labor Board, among other statements, has the following:

"Labor cannot be freed from the economic laws which likewise affect the earnings of capital."

The word "earnings," occurring in the Labor Board's statement, means "profit." It is the keynote to the Labor Board's findings. The matter of profit alone controlled the Labor Board's action. "Profit" was the basis for measuring the increasing accumulations of the capitalist on one side of a controversy to get it from labor on the other side. The State Department emphasized the findings of the Labor Board by first calling on the military forces and then on the courts to give aid to the capitalist contention. The government action of course was supposed to be predicated on the rights of the public, but the government nevertheless by its action supported the rule to compensate dead capital—capital accumulated from the past energy of the workers—to an extent which, if followed to the end, would sacrifice humanity to property holders. The whole proceeding emphasized the legal guarantee of profit to the capitalist—while the worker has no guarantee. On the contrary, the worker is forced to earn the profit for the capitalist to increase the capitalist's capital. This could not be done under the attempted readjustment plan except by a cut in wages, or by taking it from the consumer, and since the workers in the aggregate consume the most it simply would catch them the other way around.

Under the plan of the Labor Board, which is the capitalist plan and supported by law, the workers see their ultimate ruin. Every dollar added to capital is a dollar taken from labor, whether farm labor or wage labor, or small business labor, and immediately becomes another dollar for capital to receive additional profits upon. It compounds the toll of capital and correspondingly decreases the pay to the workers.

Since all capital is taken from labor in some form, the net result on the entire business and industrial system of compounding profits is to continually lessen the part of the worker's earnings that he can keep.

The extreme ultimate penalty to the workers of the false practice that has been followed has been delayed by improved machinery and improved ways to produce. The new ways have given the workers some luxuries in life which they would not otherwise have had. The effect also is to give still greater accumulated capital to the capitalist, which becomes a charge to the workers for additional profits upon that. In the end the worker often loses even from the improved conditions for production.

V

THE CAPITALISTIC AIM

The capital of the railroads already approximates 20 billions, including water. With the other capitalists' trusts, and the other wealth controllers, the total is rapidly approaching if it has not already reached 200 billions, the profits on which, when compounded on the basis of present law enforcement and established practices, will soon take all the earnings of all the workers—except what must be allowed for bare subsistence. Of course, capital does not seek to destroy the worker—farmer or other—any more than a farmer would destroy his team. Capital would itself be destroyed if it did that, but it will make labor the slave on the very rules and practices that are now followed and supported by law. It seeks to enslave and not to destroy.

When one or more labor groups strike, it is not alone a question of whether or not the strikers' wages are as good as the earnings of workers in other occupations. The real question is, shall farm labor or other labor allow the capitalist to increase capital by taking it from the workers, and if so, how much? It involves a fundamental principle. We must not let our temporary personal interest cloud our minds or prevent us from seeing beyond the present. If some workers—farm or other—supinely submit to the privilege of capital to enslave humanity, that furnishes no reason why the rest of us should submit. The plan of the capitalists now in control and in complete operation is rushing us on with ever-increasing profit to capital and corresponding loss to the useful workers.

The present system is wrong when taken in its application to labor. Nevertheless, it is capital's fortress, but an unsafe one for capital itself. For it is not constructed on a permanent plan: it is self-destructive by breeding its own opposition from fundamentally stronger forces; that is, the toilers. The world is already puzzling how to fix it. It cannot be fixed without fundamental changes—changes that the capitalists now oppose, but which are less drastic than others which are sure to result from the capitalistic opposition to anything remedial now proposed. The main trouble now is in what the law defines or permits as "reasonable profit." Upon the fallacy of so-called "reasonable profit" future wars are not unlikely to be waged. In such wars, capital will not win, because what has been called "reasonable" is unreasonable and always impossible in the end.

Superficial students make themselves believe that things can be made right by fixing a minimum wage for the employee, and a minimum price for the farmer to get for his farm product. Suppose it be done. We have already observed that under existing practice we must both buy and sell through trusts. That being so, a minimum wage pay and a minimum price to the farmer for his products allow the trust to add to the price, when the products of wage and the farm are sold back to the consumer, the full cost to the trust plus their so-called "reasonable profit." That is, it will be added to the price of life's necessaries, plus another profit to the trusts. Both farmer and wage worker get caught. If a minimum price on farm product and a minimum wage are set, as now demanded, the farmer and wage worker will continue to be exploited.

Superficial politicians cry for the minimum wage, and minimum pay to the farmer for his product, without figuring prices more than one way. When they see their blunder in not making a complete survey of the economic field, and after the people have suffered from the blunder, these superficial politicians will follow with a demand that, in addition to fixing a minimum wage and a minimum price on farm product to be paid to the farmer, a limit price be set for the farmer and wage worker to pay for the necessaries of life. Then the present economic farce would be exposed: the two prices would soon conflict with the so-called reasonable profit over which an economic blunder has already been made by the courts in regard to its measure. Reasonable profit would strike a snag.

Capital could not last long as a profiteering scheme if it were made to meet an honest minimum in buying, and an honest maximum in selling. In such cases capital would soon fall from the supremacy which it now occupies. It would not be destroyed, however, but it would be forced to hold the economic position which it should have—to serve and not to enslave mankind. We could then work to adjust the differences between the different groups of workers, not that we could secure absolute justice, but we could avoid following a scheme of certain injustice, such as our existing scheme is.

No statesman will lose much time in a stumble over the maximum and minimum price proposals. Those proposals, if tried, may serve to expose a false economy, but not to permanently settle economic differences.*

The "reasonable profit" on vested capital, as it is called, is what seals the downfall of every nation, unless a new and reasonable rule for application shall be established. It is not reasonable, according to present rulings. And reasonable profit to trusts differs sharply from the living wage and the reasonable profit that

*I make no objection to either a minimum wage or a minimum price to the farmer for his farm product, but I do insist that it is no remedy for either the wage worker or farmer. It does not go to their real trouble. I do however favor taking such action till a fundamental plan can be applied, and also because the people demand it.

they allow to workers. It is legal piracy as now applied. It is a simple thing to understand, but in spite of that fact not many understand it. The rule of "reasonable profit" is mainly responsible for the havoc played with our own economic system, yet the rule goes almost uncontested, scarcely protested. Protests are made against the effect and not against the cause.

Already profit has mounted until approximately four-fifths of all the wealth that God created in our country—plus a like proportion of what the toil of men and women have added —is now owned by the few who never earned it, that is, the profiteers. What the few over-rich own or control was adroitly secured by exploiting the masses and defrauding the government. Most of that wealth is needed to serve mankind. It is the *need of all the people* for what the few control that permits the owners to exploit the users.

The extra toll or cost, collected because of this great need and considered an element in values, is no part of the property, no property right. It is merely a condition of the users who must have the use of the property. Their condition, which is no property right, should never form an element to increase the price. It is, however, the very thing that is seized upon to exploit the users. Price should always be determined by the human energy required to produce and deliver service, whatever the service may be to the consumer, and should do justice to the producer and consumer alike so far as human rule can bring that about.

The owners loan into use money or other property—capital, as it is called—in order to secure a profit upon it. They require that it shall be kept in as good condition as when loaned; or, in case that cannot be done, then the wear and tear shall be made good by compensation. That is quite right and natural. If it stopped at that the world would be safe to live in.

In addition to keeping borrowed property intact so it may be returned to the owners as good as when loaned, or the wear and tear made good by extra compensation to the owner, the law establishes the privilege for its owners to charge profit for its use. If it is money loaned, the profit is called interest. If it is money or property invested in corporate stock, it is called dividend. If it is land or houses, the profit is called rent.

The word "profit" covers all kinds of extra compensation. The word may indicate interest or rent or anything given for the use of property that makes for the owner more wealth. No matter what we call it, profit is an extra charge by the owner to be paid by the user. It is an increase of capital to the owner and a decrease to the user unless the latter can switch the loss to others. In the aggregate result on the economic system, it amounts to a gain by the owners and a loss by the users. The users pay and the owners receive.

In the nature of things—that is, the higher law—there is no such thing as profit in the sense that capitalists figure profit. In nature there is natural growth like the forests, the grass on which herds graze, the coal that drives industry. In addition, we have production by labor in improving or assisting the natural things, and sometimes building new. Natural production and production by labor are the only ways to add to the world's wealth.

Property acquired by any other than by the natural way, through growth or by labor, academically considered, is taken from labor wrongfully even though it be acquired legally. That statement must be taken liberally, for we have no high degree of perfection in the business inter-relations of people. Some of the practices of the human family that are inconsistent with the principles of nature are the result of incapacity of the human family to adjust to natural laws those practices considered justified to meet the necessities. These practices have been overworked, however, and made to serve greed rather than to fit the requirements of an imperfect people.

We cannot go so far as to condemn all profit. The human animal is not yet a perfect human. He works better if he can have the inducement of profit. He has not reached the control over his own destiny to enable him to establish rules such as seem ideal to pure reason dissociated with mankind in action. He has, however, reached to where he can do much better than he is doing now, and it is to that end we should all seek to interest ourselves in the common welfare.

VI

CLASSIFICATION OF PROPERTY RELATIONS

It is exaggerated profit to the few taken from the masses that unsettles the world and destroys all business equilibrium. It creates industrial slaves of us. We have risen above consenting to American slave service, which the present profit exaggeration amounts to. A re-adjustment of our present business relations with each other to adjust them to our present intelligence is the only thing that will do. That much must be done. Once we understand what the present measure of profit to the super-rich means in loss to us, the present profit evil is going to be radically changed.

If we classify the people with relation to each other in their property interests, it should give a clear idea of the way we are headed and of the fact that we must face about. For that purpose we may now be classed in two groups. One group consists of those whose excess wealth is applied for the use of others and for which use profits are charged. The other group is those who have no wealth, or have some property and use it for themselves, but receive no profit. It is merely used for their own convenience. Those who have no property, for the purpose of illustration, are in this last group, because they belong to the non-profit group. Those in this group who have no property simply live from hand to mouth and are forced to pay profit to someone for everything they use. The non-profit group owns approximately 50 billions in property value, the wear and tear on which, with taxes, amounts to more than any profit collected. The profit group owns about 200 billions in property value which the law and practice recognizes as entitled to profit when used in any form to give service to others.

We will use the figure six per cent to carry out the illustration, for that will accord with a common understanding, though we are being forced to pay more than six per cent. The figure, low though it is compared with many profiteering schemes, is used as a basis to prove that the scheme is fundamentally wrong and is due for a breakdown.

The ultimate breakdown which will follow, if we do not correct things soon, is illustrated by the following diagram. Those having non-income property, including those who own no property, and those who have income property, as indicated by a diagram showing the contrast:

This space represents what 98 per cent. of the people own in property, or $50,000,000,000. It is not divided, interest, rent or other profit property. It is property used by the owners. The majority included in this class have no property.

This space represents property now owned by only 2% of the people, or $200,000,000,000. The law recognizes the owners as entitled to collect dividends or other profit when used in service. Even 6% compounded in the usual business way will double this space so as to represent $400,000,000,000 in about 11 years. That means that the 98% of the people represented in the upper space will have to pay that $200,000,000,000 increase. It will be taken out of the price of farm products, out of the wage workers' envelope and partly from the buyers of the necessaries of life by increasing the price fixed for them.

Eleven years from now, under the rule, the non-income property owners will not have materially increased their property ownership. What is more discouraging, they will be forced to earn enough in addition to what they earn now to pay profits on $200,000,000,000 additional capital—or on $400,000,000,000 then—as compared with profits on $200,000,000,000 now.

The proportion will then be as follows:

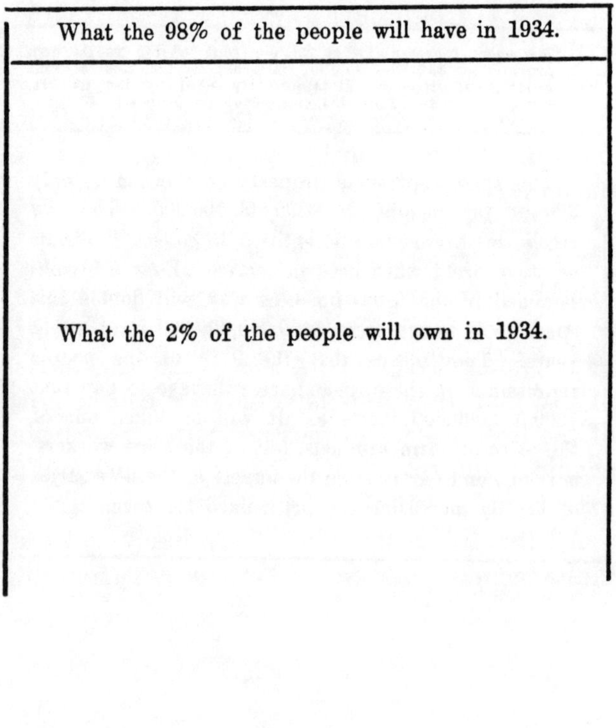

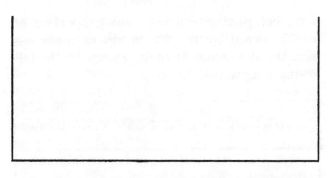

The 2% group have several ways to further exploit the 98% group and make the latter pay for doubling the profiteers' wealth in the coming 11 years. One way is to reduce the price paid the farmer for his product and also reduce the wage paid to the wage worker; another is to charge both farmer and wage worker more for the necessaries of life that they must buy; another is to force the farmer and wage worker to produce more, do more work, work more hours, and get along with less of the necessaries of life than they now have, and of course none of the luxuries sometimes permitted now. Mechanical improvements may, to some slight extent, affect these calculations.

All the different methods are likely to be simultaneously followed. To our children just born, before they can vote, the proportion of wealth owned by the 2% group as measured with the 98% group is easily shown by the following diagram:

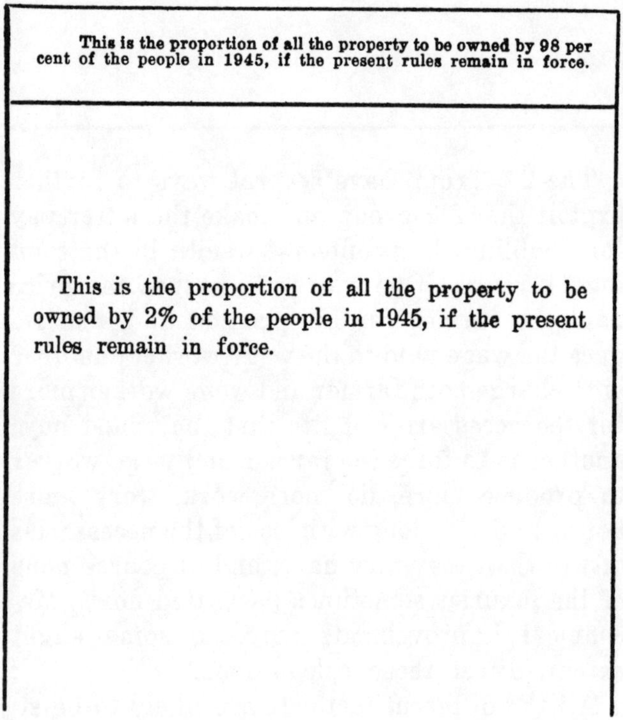
This is the proportion of all the property to be owned by 98 per cent of the people in 1945, if the present rules remain in force.
This is the proportion of all the property to be owned by 2% of the people in 1945, if the present rules remain in force.

The Standard Oil Company of New Jersey, in addition to its regular dividend (October, 1922), declared a stock dividend that year of 400 per cent. It makes the capitalization of that one corporation 500 millions. With that as an initial stock upon which to compute dividends at the same rate, compounded annually, there is only enough wealth in the country now to pay their dividends to the year 1930. They would have it all then. Of course there are not many 400 per cent profit institutions, but just the same our basis of operation carries out that principle for exploiting the people by enormous profit on material things, and sometimes on mere "watered stock" as it is called. It is a plan that enslaves us, except the lucky few who happen to possess the means or schemes with which to compel the rest of us to pay. We have already arrived at the point where property or capital—whether it is material or water, coined or put into certificates—holds a higher position in law than human beings. It outlaws humanity, and outlaws the Constitution.

Will the proud American people continue to submit to the rule that takes us with constantly increasing speed to the conditions depicted? Who thinks that we can by law stop strikes, while by unreasonable laws we force strikes? Who thinks we can stop crime by increasing the severity of punishment, if we force industrial slavery? When we drive man to the point where death is preferable to his earthly lot, he is not unlikely to give his life, if need be, for any change that seems expedient. Mankind will rise to a new freedom when there is no longer a belief in the present impossible economic plan. We should know the truth, explained by the facts.

We cannot stop strikes by law as long as capital has the existing system and the guarantee of so-called reasonable profit. The word "reasonable," used as it is, is a misnomer. The guarantee of profit will keep up trouble. We can have no permanent peace while labor is forced to slave for what amounts to a guarantee of profit, such as was allowed by the Esch-Cummins Act, and is sanctioned by the Federal Reserve Act and other laws.

Strikes are usually rebellions against wrong conditions. To avoid strikes, we must take steps to correct the conditions. Those steps direct us to considerations and acts that take place in Washington, the capital of our nation, where most of the important laws are made.

VII

THE PRESS, AND OTHERS

A well-balanced but prejudiced editorial, quoted from a capitalists' paper, runs as follows:

"Portents of the Railroad Strike.

"If there isn't some back-tracking, commonly called 'crawfishing,' in the railroad strike controversy, there will be interesting developments of another sort.

"The Railway Labor Board, true to an admonition by its chairman a few days ago, has hurled a challenge at the striking shopmen by declaring their organization outlawed and dispossessed of any further rights before the Board. The statement invited new organizations of shopmen who may take the places of the strikers so that railroad labor may be represented in disputes before the Board.

"The strike leader, B. M. Jewell, hurls the challenge straight back at the Board, saying that the Board has outlawed itself instead of the strikers' organization, that the strikers consider themselves under no further obligation to the Board, and that they are prepared to pilot themselves toward a satisfactory settlement.

"Railway executives here and there are issuing a few 'defis' on their own account. Some of them have served notice on the men who left their employ that if they do not return to work not later than today, they will lose all their seniority rights and pension privileges. Others have gone so far as to say that strikers will not be taken back under any circumstances.

"On the face of things, these three attitudes seem to set up a status of war to the finish. The Board's announcement is abrupt and directly to the point, but not more so than the reply from the strikers' chief. The railroad executives, too, are blunt and understandable.

"The Railway Labor Board is, of course, subject to a higher power. What it has ruled is true for the reason that the Board is a creature and servant of the government. Neither the Board nor the government can coerce the strikers to go back to work against their wills. It is up to the strikers themselves to decide whether they shall work for the wage specified and the conditions stipulated, but the Board chairman admonishes them that it is not theirs to say whether or not other men shall take the places left vacant by the strike. In that admonishment the Board is sustained by legal word and legal principle.

"As to the railway executives, they are still ostensibly subject to the Labor Board. They are not so free to act on their own initiative as are the men who have laid down their shop tools. The government has a power of control and regulation over transportation that it does not have over men's labor. If, however, the Labor Board is within its authority in outlawing the strikers' organization and in denying the strikers further rights before the Board, it follows that the railroad executives have a broad discretion in the matter of further dealings with the strikers.

"Two things naturally obtrude themselves into contemplation of the present situation. One of these is the comment ascribed to White House sources a few days ago that the voice of the Railway Labor Board is the voice of the government, and the other is the dictum of the United States Supreme Court about the accountability of labor organizations in courts of law.

"All these things make the present strike exceptionally interesting from the standpoint of government."

Indeed, as the editorial states: "All these things make the present strike exceptionally interesting from the standpoint of government." The government is face to face with the government inconsistencies, and it will be so even after present strikes end, even the capitalists' press must admit it.

From the same paper and number we quote a news item. It refers to a speech delivered July 4, 1922 by a United States Senator:

"... CITING ILLINOIS TROUBLE, WARNS AGAINST TYRANNY OF LABOR

"Ocean Grove, N. J., July 4. 'Disregard for the law is the greatest problem America now faces, constituting a menace which, if unchecked, spells anarchy and ruin,' declared U. S. Senator ... in an address made today at the Ocean Grove Independence Day Celebration. Declaring his belief in the rights of labor to organize, he said:

" 'The shocking occurrences recently in the coal strike region in Illinois should arouse us to action. To quit work is a right, but labor must understand that the right to work is just as sacred. Neither tyranny of capital nor tyranny of labor will be tolerated in America.' "

The Senator who made the speech voted for the Esch-Cummins Railway Act and other acts that make the capitalist supreme in forcing tyranny upon the workers everywhere. By that same Senator's vote, along with other legislators' votes, additional seed for anarchy was sown into our economic field and took deep root, which if not weeded out will grow into widespread anarchy in spite of the best of human intentions. It is a pity that the public does not have true information, so that it might understand orators who adroitly shield themselves under inconsistencies which are not apparent to their audiences except when their previous acts are made known.

Workers are forced to strike by the very laws that enjoin them from striking. The law that gives any group, official, industrial or capitalistic, power to crush labor, is a direct challenge that forces anarchy. The law itself that places commerce and the industries of the country in control of exclusive capitalist organizations and says that the profits now pratically guaranteed are reasonable, when in fact they are unreasonable and extortionate, spells anarchy and ruin unless changed. Those upon whom the burden falls rebel in self-preservation.

As things now stand, all workers are expected

by the capitalists to continually submit to having more and more of their earnings taken from them to be added to the capitalist group holdings. Eventually there will be only enough left to keep them fit to work, as a farmer keeps his team—but with less thought of them than of the team. The capitalist does not have to buy a new worker when the old is dead. The new worker comes for his feed and keep.

There are things taking place that are impossible to be continued in business. Changes must be made to save us from the ultimate fate of the old Roman Empire and of other decadent nations. There is too much that takes place that the intelligent and self-respecting people cannot be satisfied with. The complaints stated in the Declaration of Independence are examples showing when the breaking point comes to the self-respecting. If we take into account the conditions of the people, we see more injustice imposed by the profiteers and politicians of these times than is stated in the Declaration of Independence against the Imperial Government we were then under.

The fathers of that period had no means for correction except by petition or force. They exhausted the first without relief, and then applied the second. Different from our fathers—thanks to them—we have the means for correction without applying force. Still we have resorted to petition rather than applying more practical ways. We have petitioned legislative bodies for laws to be enacted and enforced to secure just results in business. The petitions have been pigeonholed without action or, in a few cases acted upon, still more impossible conditions have been imposed.

Originally there was some freedom of action, even among profiteers and politicians. If we saw fit to humiliate ourselves by allowing them to control, we could appeal to competing groups of either, and get at least some favor over what we got when we did nothing. Originally there was competition to secure political and business favors, for group advantage. There were groups—strong groups with material differences that were fighting among themselves for supremacy. There is no material difference now in the old political parties, except which shall control patronage. The profiteers too are agreed among themselves and the leading public officials, to exact as much as possible from the workers and consumers. The combination between the profiteers and the old party leaders is so complete that scattered exceptions have never been strong enough to favorably influence any results for the people.

Remedy has been attempted by alternately shifting from one to the other of the old political parties. It has been done so many times without substantial benefit that it has become a farce. Voters must realize that the old party leaders shout the ideals the people had in the original formation of the parties. Party leaders do that for propaganda purposes only. They proclaim good, and do evil. They invent all sorts of words and phrases and adopt platforms, all of which are not so bad in themselves, so far as they go, but are simply used as propaganda to fool the voters. In practice, not only are the ideals deserted but they are flagrantly violated.

The frequent panics forced upon the people are created by manipulation for the benefit of profiteers. Between panics we have what in comparison are called "good times." But times are never as good as they would be if business were done in the easiest and most proper way.

When a panic seems to be ended the people start in to build up again, thinking to profit by what they learned in the squeeze. But most of us learn nothing by panics except that we are hit severely. Just how and by whom we are hit, comparatively few of us know.

Before reviewing certain acts, it is well to observe the plan of the capitalists as stated in an article of thirty years ago. It was not intended for the public, but was propaganda to hold the big bankers together:* The article was as follows:

"We (meaning the bankers) must proceed with caution and guard every move made, for the lower order of the people are already show-

*It was in 1912 that the writer first saw this editorial. It purported to have been published in the June, 1892, number of a bankers' magazine. I investigated to see if such an article had actually been published as stated, in the June issue. I was unable to locate it in June number. In the early nineties bankers became frightened by the silverites and discussed the subject of bi-metalism in radical terms. Whether the article referred to did or did not appear is not so material as the facts and subsequent events conclusively proved that the international bankers were then and now are in the conspiracy stated in the article, and that so far their plans have succeeded.

ing signs of restless commotion. Prudence will therefore show a policy of apparently yielding to the popular will until our plans are so far consummated that we can declare our designs without fear of any organized resistance.

"The Farmers' Alliance and Knights of Labor organizations in the United States should be carefully watched by our trusted men, and we must take immediate steps to control these organizations in our interest or disrupt them.

"At the coming Omaha convention to be held July 4 (1892), our men must attend and direct its movement, or else there will be set on foot such antagonism to our designs as may require force to overcome. This at the present time would be premature. We are not yet ready for such a crisis. Capital must protect itself in every possible manner through combination and legislation.

"The courts must be called to our aid, debts must be collected, bonds and mortgages foreclosed as rapidly as possible.

"When through the process of law the common people have lost their homes, they will be more tractable and easily governed through the influence of the strong arm of the government applied by a central power of imperial wealth under the control of the leading financiers. People without homes will not quarrel with their leaders.

"History repeats itself in regular cycles.

This truth is well known among our principal men who are engaged in forming an imperialism of the world. While they are doing this, the people must be kept in a state of political antagonism.

"The question of tariff reform must be urged through the organization known as the Democratic Party, and the question of protection with reciprocity must be forced to view through the Republican Party.

"By thus dividing the voters, we can get them to expend their energies in fighting over questions of no importance to us, except as teachers to the common herd. Thus, by discrete action, we can secure all that has been so generously planned and successfully accomplished."

. . .

The facts stated in the foregoing article are only too true. We have a tremendous responsibility to overcome the imposition of imperial wealth. For more than sixty years the odds have been tremendously against us. While we have been fighting over questions of no importance to the wealthy, electing men to Congress because they claimed to belong to a political party which we happened to favor, irrespective of party these Congressmen have passed numerous bills for the benefit of profiteers, giving them the opportunity to exploit us through such measures as the Federal Reserve Bank Act and the Esch-Cummins Railway Act.

Even before the acts named became law, the profiteers were protected by legislation and combination of trusts. But wealth demanded even more than the strong arm the government had previously given. Through Congressmen whom the voters elected and through other public officials, the wealth group got possession of natural resources like water-powers, minerals, forests, etc. But the greatest of all public gifts were the new bank act and the new railway act.

VIII

BELIEVING + VOTING — THINKING

All things demonstrate what happens when we accept the kept press falsehoods for truth, believe in the adroit schemes of the wealthy and listen with open mouths to the speeches of Congressmen whose statesmanship consists in sacrificing their constituents in return for the kept press support and good committee appointments, and having the privilege of naming their political chums to fat office—these in turn telling us whom and what to vote for.

We see the national catastrophe when we measure the work of these Congressmen—some of them called "Grand Old Men." They have served grandly and long the demands of the profiteers. The misfortunes of the people and the peril of the nation are too solemn for jest; but in spite of the catastrophe the pretended wise and good Congressmen, their pompous parade for our votes and our blind following, make us look like huge jokes when we analyze *their* acts and measure them by *our* votes.

Congressmen look at each other wise-like—they present the wink of an inner secrecy. The power of the profiteers to make such "ten-strikes" as some of the laws give them, brands these Congressmen with a seal of either child-like innocence, criminal negligence or treason.

If that is not so, let us look at ourselves. We may ask the question, are we, the people, justly dealt with in that way? We selected them as our officials, and have very little knowledge of what they should do. Most of what we know is that things are not right, and most of us don't even know why they are not right. We just know that they are not, and we want them to be right. We do not tell the officials what we want done as a rule. We just criticise what has been done and the things that are and expect the officials to correct what we criticise—without telling them how. Our exploiters tell them how they want things done, and how to avoid doing what we want done without explaining that it is avoidance. Maybe we deserve things to be as they are because of our failures. That we must further investigate, to see.

Who, with ordinary experience, could read the Federal Reserve Bank Act or the Esch-Cummins Railway Act, and not know that in both the doors are left wide open for the profiteers to rob the people of billions of dollars?

Who with ordinary common sense, would not know from past experiences of the profiteers that when the doors are left open to rob us, they do rob us?

Several of the acts of Congress unmistakably show upon their face the opportunity presented for profiteers to force the masses into bankruptcy only to pile up more wealth for the already over-rich. Not only does Congress make gifts one after the other to the profiteers, in the way of legislation, the granting of special privileges, but Congressmen in their obedience to the system recommend for appointment judges and other public officials,* charged with

*The Federal judges are appointed for life. Therefore we are tied to the old judicial order. The people themselves may become so well informed concerning their rights that public opinion based on justice—not on temporary expediency—will influence the judicial temperament to reason from the side of supporting human permanency and independence, rather than from the side of property,

the duty of interpreting and administering the acts of Congress. All things work to the same end—the strong arm of government dominated by profiteers.

The voters repudiated a leader in Congress who was instrumental in passing the Esch-Cummins Act, repudiated him because of his support of that act. The President immediately appointed that man a member of the Interstate Commerce Commission with powers to help administer the act, and the Senate confirmed the appointment—a travesty on free government. Yet that method of reward for betraying the people—if it is betrayal, and it looks like it—is a practice commonly followed. But, it seems that we expect it, for ordinarily we re-elect all the officials who make the appointments.

capital now being entitled to a super-privilege for compensation that leads to industrial slavery. If that does not happen, the only other relief will be to increase the number of judges sufficiently, and select them with a view to consistent consideration of human rights as distinguished from property privileges. The judges have been increased in number recently, but their selection has been based on the same considerations that have always governed in the past.

Evidence before Congress proved conclusively that the Federal Reserve Act was planned by Wall Street. It was clear to every Congressman who would read it that the very persons who planned it were the leaders in control of the money trust, men who dominated the business interests to the point of strangling those not in league with the exploiters. The President appointed to the Federal Reserve Board one of the most prominent of the money trust group. All of the appointive members of the Board follow the plans that exactly fit the money trust operations.

To place a farmer on the Board, as has since been done, is mere "sop to the farmers," as Congressmen often state it when they designedly play such stunts. No "dirt farmer" can sit with the other members on the Board and accomplish anything worth while for the farmers. The whole scheme is wrong.

It is a common practice of Congressmen to make the *title* of acts promise aright, but in the body or text of the acts to rob the people of what is promised in the title. The Federal Reserve Act is a conspicuous example of that practice. It starts with a lie by promising:

"An act to provide for Federal Reserve Banks to furnish an elastic currency, to afford a means of rediscounting commercial paper, to establish a more effective supervision of banking in the United States and for other purposes."

The first words of the act are definite promises which the people assumed Congress made, that the banks established were Federal Reserve—that is, *government* banks. That promise was a deliberate lie. The government does not own one dollar of stock in the Federal Reserve banks. Every word and phrase in the title of the act is an implication of good business to mankind—made so to deceive. The title to the act was intended to charm all the innocent among us. But the truth is, IT IS A SNAKE. Its head appears where we would expect to find its tail. Yet our new banks are expected to find its tail.

The last clause of the Bank Act title reads: "And for other purposes." It is for those "other purposes" mostly—purposes perpetrated on the farmers, wage workers and small businesses not associated with the trusts—that this master bank act—the Federal Reserve

Bank Act, the present guardian of all the other trusts—is administered. We have seen the snake's two-forked tongue, holding back for a little, encouraging as if to charm, then repeatedly striking its poison fangs into the very soul of the nation's business till that nation lay prostrate with millions of idle, underfed, discontented, would-be workers and millions of impoverished farmers. Great were the promises made from 1907 to 1920 by the exploiters, when they asked for and were given that act, but the result is dire. They will ease up on the people again, as they have done before, but only preparatory to another drive to further exploit us.

We have witnessed what happened to the people. Congress gave power to the profiteers, and what have the profiteers taken with that power? They possess the minerals of the earth; the most valuable of the forests; the best of the water-powers; the transportation systems, rail and water; and the banks with entire control of money and credit. In fact, the profiteers possess all the natural resources and the industrial and commercial appliances that are capable of trust control. These properties are what is called "capital," forming the basis on which to collect profit.

Congress practically guarantees interest, dividends and rents; the courts order that we must pay them. We are delivered into industrial slavery under the seal of the law—the military in reserve to enforce it. God pity our children, for unless they compel the recognition of their rights better than we present voters have done, they will be borne down with added burdens of increased wealth in profiteers' hands to command and compound still greater interest, dividends and rents.

How all this could take place, when not long ago we owned the natural resources to which our working intelligence and drudgery have added the rest, would seem a mystery if we did not know it has been the work of politicians and high officials in their deliberate betrayal of the people by giving special privilege to a few thousand to exploit a hundred million other Americans.

The people have cried out for reform, cried out for corrections, held scores of elections, alternately trying one set of officials then another, each failing, trying it over again and still failing, trying still others—but all the time the people have found themselves deeper and deeper in debt* to the few who produce nothing, but nevertheless already own four-fifths of all that God has created, as well as what men and women have added by their toil. Imperial wealth knew what it wanted and got what it wanted by going after it through the legislatures, Congress, the executives and public officials generally. The process was to persistently demand what it wanted, and to fool the people to elect those who gave it to them.

Office-holders understand that by joining with the interests to exploit the people, their re-election is more certain than if they serve the people who elect them. By joining the exploiters their campaign expenses are paid, the support of the "machines" and the capital press is assured, and if by chance they should

*If we borrow from a bank and give our note, we call it debt. There is a chance for us to pay that debt. The bank would not give us the loan unless it believed that we would pay. But the debt they say we owe to the profiteers to pay a "reasonable profit" on what has been taken from us, in most cases dishonestly or unfairly, we never can pay by any present rule of conduct.

lose they are appointed to some office that suits them equally well or better. On the other hand, when they do support the people, as occasionally a few do, usually the voters—at the request of the profiteers—defeat such at a succeeding election and they scarcely ever land an appointive office. If they do, it is to get them out of the way so they cannot block some scheme. In some European colonies native rebels are, similarly, knighted.

The United States Chamber of Commerce is a private body; so is the International Chamber of Commerce. The latter announced that its second annual session would be held in Rome during the week of March 19, 1923. It was stated that several hundred of America's big business men will attend. The two above organizations are to complete the plan made thirty years ago, to "form an imperialism of the world under control of the leading financiers." *

*As a part of this scheme able financiers are being dispatched to different countries to prepare the way for an international banking system to bring the world under control of one money trust.

W. P. G. Harding, former Governor of the Federal

These master organizations retain the keenest of attorneys, who prepare bills, treaties and proposed measures, of different purposes, for official action. In their aid they command the support of all subsidiary associations, like local chambers of commerce and other groups that they dominate. They get practically all they demand, and they demand the things that make them masters of mankind.

Reserve Board, on October 31, 1922, left for Cuba to assist in re-organizing the finances of that island. Mr. Harding was Governor of the Federal Reserve Board during the entire period of inflation and through the first years of the deflation.

IX

BANKS AND THE PEOPLE

We are all interested in the banks whether we have direct dealings with them or not. They are convenient. No business is so well systematized to influence times and conditions as the banks. The press may mold public opinion, but the bankers direct the course of the business. The general opinion is that the bigger the bank the stronger the bank. That is a careless way to think. Most banks are financially sound, but not all. The exceptions are few. Since there are exceptions, it is well to know how to judge strength.

The borrowers determine the financial standing of a bank. If the borrowers are not good—not able to pay—then the bank is not sound. The capital of a bank cuts less figure than the borrowers' notes when it comes to financial strength. The deposits are loaned to the borrowers. The borrowers give notes—written promises—to the banks; the depositors' credits are loaned out—turned into notes—and are then merely assets, not cash.

For instance, a bank with $25,000 capital and $100,000 deposits has in assets the equivalent of $1 of capital, and $4 of deposits loaned to borrowers, to pay each $4 of deposits that it owes, or in reserve and in borrowers' notes it has $5 in assets to pay every $4 that it owes.

A bank with $100,000 capital and $800,000 deposits has in assets the equivalent of only $1 of capital, and $8 of deposits loaned to borrowers, to pay each $8 of deposits that it owes, or in reserve and in borrowers' notes only $9 in assets to pay every $8 that it owes.

A bank with $1,000,000 capital and $15,000,000 deposits has in assets the equivalent of only $1 of capital, and $15 of deposits loaned to borrowers, to pay each $15 that it owes, or in reserve and in borrowers' notes only $16 in assets to pay every $15 that it owes.*

*Each stockholder is individually liable to the depositors equal to the amount of stock he holds—that much in addition to the full payment for his stock. That does not, however, change the relative strength of the banks as described.

Generally, in addition to loaning the deposits, a part of the capital is also loaned out. The notes are simply a part of the bank's assets. The facts stated show that it is the borrowers that must prove the strength or weakness of banks. If the borrowers are solvent the bank is sound, otherwise not.

The cases cited, of course, are true examples. The small bank has assets—$5 in capital and borrowers' notes to pay every $4 that it owes; while the bank with four times as much capital and eight times as much deposits has assets—only $9 of capital and borrowers' notes to pay every $8 that it owes; and the still larger bank has assets—only $16 of capital and borrowers' notes to pay each $15 that it owes. In points of strength they rate: 120 points in favor of the small bank, $112\frac{1}{2}$ and $106\frac{2}{3}$ respectively for the two larger banks. This fact should be emphasized: the banks that make loans to responsible borrowers are sound. Advertising that a bank is strong because it is the largest is not necessarily true. It is often false.

The question of the strength of banks however is less important than the power of banks over business. Finance in the hands of the big bankers practically controls our business interests, and Europe (1923) is stranded on her problem of finance.

Banks are not organized to do business with the banks' own money. They are organized to get other people's money to do business with. Deposits are what the banks want. It is not so much deposits of real money either that concern them as it is to manipulate credits. Most of the deposits are credits, not money.

All the money in the United States, outside the Treasury in Washington, does not exceed $6,000,000,000, while the deposits in the banks approximate $40,000,000,000.

It is manipulation of credits that creates the big deposits. A person borrows $100,000, we will say. The bank takes his note, drawing interest, but gives the borrower no money—simply gives him credit on the bank's books and hands the borrower a check book. That note increases the deposits of the bank $100,000. The bank has no additional actual money by that deal. The borrower pays his bills with checks. Persons who get the checks, with rare exceptions, deposit them in the same or some other bank. Other banks do a like business, so on the average it works out about the same for all banks. It simply amounts to a transfer of bank credits from the persons giving checks to the persons receiving checks.

The above example explains in a general way why it is that the banks have 7, 8 or 10 times as many deposits as there is money. The banks use other people's credit as well as other people's money, and that is what piles up deposits.

It is a common saying that we do business on bank credit. It is nearer the truth to say that the bankers do business on borrowers' credit. If the borrower fails to pay the bank the bank would fail to pay the depositors. In times of stress banks help each other. That makes them more secure for the public also. It is a bad thing and harms innocent people when banks fail.

The banks did not originally rely on each other for a complete cooperative system to the extent they do now. The panics created by profiteers forced many banks to fail because their assets consisted of borrowers' notes and not cash. The soundness of banks depends on the borrowers being solvent, but when persons borrow they promise to pay in the future.

Most notes run from 90 days to 6 months, few longer. Those who owe notes do not have to pay till the notes come due. If the depositors start a run on a bank and all demand pay at one time, the bank can't pay all and must close unless the bank itself can borrow money.

The National Bank System, created during the Civil War, served the profiteers well, but as the nation's commerce increased with the growth of the country it became too limited to suit either the big profiteers or the people. The people objected to a profiteer system and wanted something fair to take its place. The big profiteers knew that the old banking law was their own scheme, but they wished a still bigger profit scheme. Let us see who won.

X

THE FEDERAL RESERVE ACT

In the early months of 1907 and for some time prior a great number of trusts had, by combination and other means, been formed into larger trusts. We then had what is termed "a business boom." The big profiteers saw the strain on our then financial system and knew that if they were going to keep expanding to larger dealings and bigger profits they must have not only a finance system of their own, but through it the control of all or at least most of the banks. We too were dissatisfied with the old system. We complained, but we as a people are always slow to act, if we ever do decide to act on matters of that kind.

The profiteers saw this opportunity and staged the 1907 panic. That was their way of stirring us up. The city banks refused to pay on demand of depositors—they also refused to pay in cash for checks. Many of the country banks did the same thing, were forced to because they had re-deposited a part of their funds in the city banks. The latter refused to pay the country banks in cash and the panic was on. It did not last long but it served its purpose—to stir up the people, to make them more dissatisfied with the old bank system. Secretly, the profiteers in New York and elsewhere organized headquarters in Chicago for a Citizens' League propaganda to demand a new bank system.

Speakers were sent to the cities and to most of the country towns, following the 1907 panic and up to 1913. They formed Citizens' Leagues everywhere. The people were induced to demand of Congress that "some bill" be passed to create a new banking system, just a demand that "some bill" be passed.

Wall Street had its bill all ready—drafted it in 1906. The people were suspicious of a Wall Street game. In the meantime I happened to be in Congress and, realizing the purpose of Wall Street, started the Money Trust Investigation. A money trust was proven. It manipulated finance and business on an enormous scale and strangled all enterprise that undertook in any way to compete with the money trust group. That investigation, with the time it took to make the final report, delayed the profiteers in getting the Federal Reserve Act passed. In spite of the proof set before every Congressman that it was the Wall Street scheme, Congress by an overwhelming vote passed the Federal Reserve Act, and the President signed it practically as Wall Street had planned.

The people had been suspicious that if one big central bank should be created Wall Street would control it; to fool us, the act provided twelve big banks instead of one, all owned by the member banks, but all under the control of a Federal Reserve Board with headquarters in Washington, D. C. To put the control in one central board was pleasing to Wall Street. It really gave Wall Street some advantages over one central bank by subdividing the country into districts, since the law itself gave the Federal Reserve Board the privilege of establishing different interest rates in different districts.

It is important to know the controlling feature of the Federal Reserve Bank. It controls "the times," dictates business, affects our homes and practically everything in which we are interested.

The Federal Reserve banks grabbed all the gold in the country. For each dollar of gold accompanied by eligible paper, pledged to the government as security, the Federal Reserve banks are given a direct path to Uncle Sam's Treasury to get money—Federal Reserve notes —at a cost of one-half of one per cent. That is a special privilege that no one else in the nation has, and still it is said that our country grants special privilege to none. However, this is not the only special privilege, that our laws give, as before noted. Yet perhaps the most vicious provision of the Federal Reserve Act is that permitting and directing the Federal Reserve Board to fix interest rates. By that act the Board makes times tough or easy at its own option, and can and does apply it in different degrees to the different districts, making different rates for different classes of borrowers, one rate for farm paper, another for commercial paper and so forth—arbitrarily exercised, with no remedy by appeal for its wrongs.

I was a member of the Banking and Currency Committee in the House when the Federal Reserve Act was passed. On the Committee I was the only member to strenuously oppose the act and the subsequent use of it as a whip over the people. Several times after the act was passed Congress added administrative provisions to increase the Board's powers. When the profiteers were manipulating for this I made a long speech in Congress—January 20, 1915—reviewing the original provisions of the act, opposing the entire law and any increase of power. I quote the following lines from my speech of that date:

"Congress, by the passage of the Federal Reserve Act, put into the control of the big banks . . . the means by which they may obtain information in regard to the financial standing of every subsidiary bank, railway and industrial corporation, and use such information for purposes of speculation to their enormous advantage over others not having access to the same means of information. It has placed it in the power of the Money Trust to make and determine prices of speculative and other commodities at its will.

"To cause high prices, all the Federal Reserve Board will do will be to lower the rediscount rate so that the associated banks will more generally apply for and receive the Federal Reserve notes, producing an expansion of credit and a rising stock market; then when business and business men are adjusted to these conditions, it can check . . . prosperity in mid-career by arbitrarily raising the rate of interest. It can cause the pendulum of a rising and falling market to swing gently back and forth by slight changes in the discount rate, or cause violent fluctuations by a greater rate variation, and in either case it will possess inside information as to financial conditions and advance knowledge of the coming change, either up or down. This is the strangest, most dangerous advantage ever placed in the hands of a special privilege class by any Government that ever existed. This act makes it . . . easy for the Money Trust to control banks. . . .

"The President, in creating the Federal Reserve Board, appointed men who had been educated by the Money Trust system, believed in it and knew no other. The Federal Reserve Act gives a power to the Federal Reserve banks that makes the Government impotent to protect the people until further legislation shall be had.

"Already the Federal Reserve banks have cornered the gold and gold certificates, so that these are no longer in circulation among the people. Finances generally are in the control of the big banks by authority of the Federal Reserve Act.

"The system is private, conducted for the sole purpose of obtaining the greatest possible profits from the use of other people's money, and in the interest of the stockholders and those allied with them. It is inconsistent with free government to subject every industry and enterprise in the country to the domination of the big banks which have been granted the exclusive privilege to control our finances.

"The banks have power to create panics when they please by making demand for payment of even as low as ten per cent of the obligations owing to them and by refusing to make new loans or extend old ones. By insidious means the Money Trust banks control legislation, and by that means have secured the exclusive privileges they now possess. . . . The people have not formed a complete plan to demand Congress to act on. The nation confronts a crisis. Action should at once be taken to extend to the farmers a proper rural credit system with aid from the Government. . . . The farmers, most of all, are defenseless under the present system because of the inability of the local banks to make long-time loans in sufficient amounts . . . and for the further reason that the Money Trust banks have intentionally kept the farmers from securing proper relief. . . ."

It will be noted that I stated what would take place later. It indicates how, under the law—a law that practically outlaws the Constitution and the nation—the privilege is given to the money trust to inflate and deflate the country at the pleasure of that mother of all trusts, and at the same time to call to its help the *government.* That law places the people absolutely at the mercy of the money trust.

The law provides the very means by which the money trust forces us to disclose to it our private affairs, to give it the information by which to crush us, as has been done under its provision. They know in advance when to create panics to their advantage. They also know when to stop a panic. Inflation and deflation work equally well for them when they control finance. Only the most unusual things catch them unawares. The World War was partly a surprise, but they commanded the aid of the government and quickly turned the War into the most profitable thing for them that had ever at any time taken place.

FEDERAL RESERVE SPYING

Practically everybody in business has to borrow, as well as many who are not in business. When they borrow it gives an excuse to find out all about the borrowers' personal affairs. The Federal Reserve banks have a clever way for that. They demand of the member banks a statement from the borrowers in order that the member banks may use the borrowers' notes as security for re-discounts. The following is one form letter sent out by the Federal Reserve banks to member banks:

CIRCULAR NO. 246

"When this bank was first organized, we realized that it was not the general practice for banks to secure signed statements from borrowers, and therefore for six years we have been accepting cashier's ratings on all unsecured agricultural notes for re-discount of $500 or more. Such cashier's ratings have proven in such cases extremely unsatisfactory, and inasmuch as all of the member banks in this district (the 9th district) have had ample time to bring their credit files up to date by securing signed financial statements, this letter is to advise that on and after July 1, 1921, all notes . . . offered for re-discount . . . must be accompanied by certified copy of signed financial statement of maker."

It will be noted by the above instructions that the member banks doing business with borrowers are practically forced to get statements from their borrowers.* The profiteers adroitly

*The Federal Reserve Banks want every scrap of information, which, considering that they are perfectly secure, independent of the borrowers' worth, is undoubtedly for the benefit of the big profiteers to keep the country checked up, so they may know when to inflate and deflate to their best profit schemes. In the blank that borrowers sign, the borrower answers approximately sixty questions, and in addition the borrower has a hint to chalk up his personal matters. The blank is too extensive to be reprinted here, containing about eight hundred printed words in addition to blank spaces.

The following is a sample of a letter received by a borrower from his banker, a banker whose reliability is not in the remotest way questioned:

"DEAR MR. ———

"I have your favor of 3rd inst., giving me in a rough way a statement of your financial condition. I regret to say that this will not pass the department's (referring to the Federal Reserve Bank) requirements, and I am inclosing found a plausible excuse for calling for it. The Federal Reserve banks have never lost a dollar nor been in danger of losing, but in spite of that fact make the demand on member banks. If it were not for the purpose behind it, to call for such statements would not be out of place. But those simple statements coming from all the borrowers give the money trust inside information of how to manipulate the markets against all the people. Calling for the statements, like many other things, is not in itself unreasonable, but the statements are used for improper purposes. With those statements tabulated, the profiteers know when they can press the debtors for new profiteering advantages.

Inflation and deflation are the terms used mostly to express expansion and contraction in money. Inflation creates the so-called booms,

another blank and wish you would take a few minutes to give me a detailed statement.

"These statements are checked up by the examiners on all loans of $500 or over, and I must have the statement in order to get them to pass the loan.

"Sincerely yours,

——————— *Cashier.*"

and deflation the panics. The last eleven most important panics in this country are those of 1857, 1864, 1873, 1884, 1890-91, 1893-94, 1897, 1903, 1907, 1913 and our late panic of 1921-23, which is still with us.

Panics are quite regular in recurrence under our system. The profiteers can and do create them as a profit scheme for themselves. Good or poor crops seem to have little bearing on panics except as the profiteers make use of them.

Before the Federal Reserve Act became law, the panics were not scientifically created. They were brought about in a bungling way, just forced by a combination of circumstances that the profiteers managed.

XI

PANICS NOW SCIENTIFICALLY CREATED

Under the Federal Reserve Act panics are scientifically created. The present panic is the first scientifically created one, worked out as we would figure a mathematical problem.

After a panic—rather at the tail end of a panic—everything has gone to the bottom in price except money. Money is at the very top price. A panic, in all other things and commodities, becomes a boom for money. Money is the one thing in demand by everybody, and nearly everybody throws everything else overboard to get money. Money becomes scarce to most people, for they do not get much for what they sell; besides, most have debts dragging behind them and what they get goes to pay the debts. It is after a panic has driven every commodity to the bottom and has got farmers, wage workers, the smaller business interests and small speculators all down in the dumps, discouraged, that things are again made ready for a boom.

We observed that the World War took the American profiteers somewhat by surprise. They were not quite ready for a thing like that, they did not look for it just at that time. But they are versatile and quickly got ready. Their first act was to create a panic, that is, to intensify the one already started in 1913. Everybody was keyed up by the suddenness of the war and it was to be easy picking for Wall Street, but even Wall Street was not able to meet such an emergency without the aid of Uncle Sam. That aid could be achieved the easiest by first scaring the people out of their wits.

Wall Street, with its vast banks in New York City and associated banks in all other large cities, suggested that there was prospect of the most disastrous panic that the world had known —unless Congress gave them emergency currency. The Federal Reserve Bank Act was already law but it took a long time to organize, and was not when the War started organized to do business. Therefore the profiteers, unless they got assistance from Uncle Sam, would not be able to get the bargains that were offered when Europe was forced to throw on the market five or six billion in American securities that she held against American debtors. Neither could these great, swivel-chair operators of Wall Street exploit the commerce that would follow between the war nations and our country, as a great profiteering game, unless Uncle Sam came to their aid financially—that is, would give them more currency.

Instead of aiding the people as the government should have done, Congress immediately passed an Emergency Currency Act to furnish the banks, that the speculators controlled, all the money they should need till they could operate the Federal Reserve Act. The speculators received from Uncle Sam nearly $400,000,000 under the provisions of the Emergency Currency Act, and when the Federal Reserve Act really got to operating they had nearly $4,000,000,000 at one time under that Act and could get as much more as they wanted. Of course they would use judgment about the amount, lest they defeat their own purposes. They could be depended upon so far as that was concerned.

With the Emergency Currency Act passed and the money in their hands, the Federal Reserve Act almost whipped into operation, a Federal Reserve Board, composed of Wall Street adherents, and the greatest of wars in progress across the waters—the year 1914 was the beginning of the greatest speculative boom the world has known. Following that, and still in progress, came the greatest panic the world has known. The principal operators in this great boom and the present panic are the Wall Street group. Our banking system in the hands of the operators is the mother of both the boom and the panic.

All the gold snapped up and piled up in the twelve Federal Reserve banks was the basis for inflation to start and conduct the boom. The law made a path direct from the Federal Reserve banks to the Treasury of the United States, to get money. For every $1,000 of gold with eligible paper, pledged as security, Uncle Sam gave $2,500 of paper money and charged only half of one per cent, so it can readily be seen why these Federal Reserve banks grabbed the gold. They have in their vaults now more than $3,000,000,000 of gold, and could and would stop the money stringency at once if Wall Street might make more money by doing that than by continuing the panic.

XII

THE WAR BOOM

The speculators bought the American commodities for European shipment, re-selling to the war nations at enormous profit. At first they took in part payment American securities that were held over there, getting these securities at bargain prices. The armies were destroying commodities over there, and the people were producing comparatively little, so our products were in demand, causing a tremendous demand upon our plain people to produce. The inducement for exertion on the part of our people was big wages and big prices for farm and other products. Everybody went to work to get rich except those who went to war,—heartily cheered. The profiteers could no longer keep prices down, either on wages or farm products. It took a little more money to pay these plain producers —the farmer and the wage worker. The profiteers were too busy now making great profit selling abroad to lose much time dickering or disputing with either farmer or wage worker. Instead, the profiteers and patrioteers multiplied the price to the purchasers, both domestic and foreign. The profiteers stood between the producers and the ultimate consumers, so the profiteers had no serious obstacles in pushing prices up.

It took stacks of money to handle the inflation, both for the plain producers and for the profiteers. It was the scheme of the Federal Reserve Act to supply the money, under control of Wall Street as the guardian of booms and panics and for the benefit of itself. The government furnished the money to the Federal Reserve banks, the Federal Reserve banks loaned to the member banks, and the member banks loaned to the trade—to the people.

To induce more borrowing from the Federal Reserve banks, to boost inflation, the Federal Reserve Board encouraged the member banks by fixing low rates of interest for member banks to pay for re-discounts, so member banks could re-loan at very good profit. The Federal Reserve banks could pledge stacks of gold, which they had plucked from the country, to Uncle Sam and get 2½ of paper for 1 of gold, and pay only one-half of one per cent to Uncle Sam for the money.

Of course, the member banks do not get the money at one-half per cent from the Federal Reserve, but must pay whatever rate of interest the Federal Reserve Board directs. When the Wall Street group so wishes, the interest rate is made low so as to induce member banks to borrow, and afterward high when they are wanted to pay up. The law places no limit on the member banks as to what they may charge the plain borrowers. The banks may stumble on usury laws, but as they understand these it gives them no trouble.

The purpose of that Wall Street plan was to continually inflate prices during the war and for a few months following. Gold was used as a basis to inflate money. The member banks pledged their customers' notes, given for loans, to the Federal Reserve banks and the latter in turn pledged to Uncle Sam this paper and forty per cent in gold as security for Federal Reserve notes—the kind of money mostly in use now. In November, 1920, the Federal Reserve banks had *at one time* $3,588,713,000 of this money for which they paid Uncle Sam one-half of one per cent. That sum was more than half of all the money in the country, so it is seen how powerful the Wall Street group was to control the times. Everybody had been expanding to the limit, borrowing at rates of interest lower than had been common, so farmers, wage workers, small business interests, even country banks, were working at high speed, little expecting Wall Street to ring up the 1920-22 panic.

XIII

WAR DEFLATION

Before Wall Street commenced the new panic it conceived the idea of hitting the farmers extra hard, because by so doing the profiteers would scalp a few extra billions' profit. Wall Street, knowing things to be in its control, got more and more bold and became stronger and stronger, intrenched by laws drafted and administered to its own exclusive liking. But the time had come to deflate, to deflate before the farmer marketed the crop that had cost so much money and strength to produce. The Wall Street group had made billions, and these billions would not be worth so much if the money could not be used to buy cheaper. Now was the time to boom money, and not goods, the Wall Street group decided. It had created a dollar that it got cheap and now would make it dear.

The Federal Reserve Board was called upon to execute the trick. It began by raising the interest rate to member banks, borrowing from the Federal Reserve banks and notifying member banks to collect part of the notes due them, and to help retire some of the outstanding Federal Reserve notes. A part of the money in circulation and in the banks was to be taken from us in that way. The Federal Reserve Board at once began pressing the campaign of deflation harder and harder, raising the re-discount rate to member banks more and more, cutting off credit and commanding the member banks not to extend credit, but instead to collect their notes. Farmers wholesale began to sell crops below cost of production to pay their debts.

As a part of the profiteer plan the Esch-Cummins law was enacted. The Interstate Commerce Commission fixed the tariffs under the act, and made freight rates so high that it materially decreased the price paid to the farmer for his farm product and increased the cost to the consumer. It had like effect on the wage workers' product, decreasing the wages paid and increasing the cost of the product to the consumer. The producers and consumers, mostly farmers and wage workers, generally live so far apart that this difference in the price paid to the producer and cost to the consumer, caused by higher freight rates, made it disastrous to the producer and prohibitive to the consumer. In many cases transportation charges will exceed the price paid the farmer and other producers. Even this does not take into account other middlemen who also must have their profit when business is done.

The direct consequence of that policy, together with the money panic drive, put more than 5,000,000 wage workers out of jobs, during the winter of 1921-22, and caused the farmers to slacken their producing work. Soup lines had to be established in the cities to save the lives of idle wage workers and others dependent on the heads of families out of employment.

Under the Federal Reserve and the Esch-Cummins Acts it was easy for those in control to drive the panic as hard as they wished. The panic found the people in possession of billions in Liberty Bonds. Those the profiteers now wanted. They were too busy making profits at the time they were issued to buy many then. They bought just enough to get across with the pretense that they were "loyalists." For they knew the plan for seizing the bonds later at a bargain, in the same way they had grabbed up the American securities held across the waters when the War started. The press had originally run propaganda claiming that not only should the Liberty Bonds be subscribed by everybody as a matter of loyalty, but that as additional inducement they would be a wonderful investment. The bonds were safe, of course, as safe as any obligation can be. The nation would pay them, but for persons who had to borrow to buy they were certainly no inducement as a money investment, for the borrower would have to pay a larger rate of interest than the bonds draw. Nevertheless, the good people borrowed money to buy Liberty Bonds. When the panic came they hung tenaciously to the bonds until the stress of the panic forced them finally to sell. These bonds that had cost them one hundred cents on the dollar, plus interest on money borrowed with which to pay for the bonds, they were now forced to sell—many of them for less than eighty-five cents on the dollar. This again made additional billions for the profiteers, for just as soon as they got the bonds the value went back to one hundred cents on the dollar; and is more than that at this writing.

When the war was going on, and just following, many obligations such as municipal bonds, bonds and mortgages of industrial and other corporations, and of individuals to the extent of billions of dollars, had come due and had to be renewed. Besides, all kinds of improvements, except those necessary for the prosecution of the war, ceased during that period. Every energy was put forth to win the war, so now a vast amount of bonds and indebtedness would be contracted to finance new works, as well as to renew the old unpaid indebtedness. By bringing on the panic at this time, all these obligations for future payment were made to command higher rates of interest, and since they run for long periods—some of them possibly fifty years—here again the profiteers scalp additional billions from us and our children. In plain words we and our children have the mortgage on our backs.

XIV

ULTIMATE BREAKDOWN, OR RADICAL CHANGE

All in all, the boom of commodity prices and the fall of the purchasing power of money from 1914 to the beginning of the panic, and then the fall of commodity prices except those controlled by the trusts, with the sharp increase of the purchasing power of money during the panic following the boom, creates a condition for a future boom in the interests of the profiteers, temporarily easing up on the people, if "the radicals" do not scare it away.

Our future and the future of our children have been doubly mortgaged by the wonderful profiteering schemes of the last eight years, mortgaged on a larger scale than ever before. It is simply a larger installment of the great profiteering game, growing in its burdens all the time and forcing us into greater and greater debt, debt that can never be paid under the present system of finance; but, on the contrary, will increase until by its own excesses it breaks down by forcing its own repudiation. It cannot much longer stand the strain imposed by its own plan. However, if we in sufficient numbers ever understand the hopelessness of it, it may be so reconstructed as to liquidate and rebuild in the interest of all the people.

It is plain that our financial system is *wrong.* It is equally plain that it controls business, and that because of that control business is in bad shape. The financial system never was right, but it is now the most burdensome ever. It has been turned over to a little board, previously referred to, called the Federal Reserve Board. That board administers the finance system by authority of the government in the interest of a purely profiteering group. The board is not elected, but appointed by the President. The people are helpless before that board, for they cannot recall it.

It should not be too obscure for the bankers to see that a system, so utterly wrong as the existing banking system, cannot last. Their own future is at stake. The system is scientific, to be sure, but in the temporary interest of the big bankers only, and dangerous to the small bankers even now. The system must be changed to operate scientifically in the interest of all the people. If not, disaster will be the result, not only to the people but to the bankers as well.

Correction of the financial system is not difficult to plan, but whatever plan may be adopted it will be opposed by the profiteers, and the administration of an honest plan, at first, will be made difficult by their opposition. Dire things will be prophesied. Even though the contracts of the past are not just to this or any future generation, it is possible to carry out those contracts, provided that all new obligations are put upon a scientific and an honest basis.

The reason that it is possible to carry out the old contracts,* if we establish an honest and

*The moral or immoral aspect of repudiation is not considered here. The obligation of future generations to uphold the tainted obligations of their ancestors might furnish a subject for deep discussion. Whether the innocent purchaser of tainted bonds, stocks, and other things is as innocent as the unborn babes who will be called upon in due time to make payment, has some latitude when it comes to discussion from the viewpoint of pure morals. The question of expediency in the matter is another problem.

scientific system to govern all future engagements and contracts, is that even now—large as the material concentrated wealth has become—it is insignificant when compared with the true product of labor. Most of what is produced is consumed within a short time after production. Production must continually go on, or the world go down. That is why labor will always have the power of mastery when it becomes intelligently directed.

Groups of farmers repeatedly appeared before Congress, for practically two generations before the passage of the Federal Reserve Act, asking for a rural credit system, but were turned down with the common remark that it was special legislation and therefore could not be given. What the farmers requested was not even as special as what Congress had already repeatedly given to the banks and other trusts. The farmers never ceased their bombardment of Congress for a rural credit system, however often turned away without action.

Finally, when Congress passed the Federal Reserve Act giving to the big bankers the greatest special privilege that had ever been given to any group, the farm group cited that fact and pressed with renewed vigor for a rural credit system. Congress could no longer dodge on the ground of having no power to grant "special privilege," so the Congressmen got together to see what they could give to the farmers that the big bankers would not object to. The officers of the American Bankers' Association got busy to influence the Finance Committee in the Senate and the Banking and Currency Committee in the House to get up something which would mollify the farmer and at the same time do as little as possible to interfere with the control of even the farmers' finance by the big banks. They finally got up the existing law on farm credits. Do you suppose this useful group—the farmers—were given a direct path to the treasury of Uncle Sam to get money at any price? "Not on your life." They were given a law through the operation of which, by cumbersome methods, the farmers may borrow some money on their farms. It is a long way around, and takes a long time for a farmer to get money through the rural credit system, and it has not lessened his burden much. Those in charge are making it difficult and slow to get money through the farm credit law.

No group of workers is more useful than the farm group, but the bankers were given special privilege to control finance and business, while the farmers were refused even a fair, workable rural credit system. The bankers got what they asked for and more than they expected, while the farmers got nothing that relieves them of their greatest burden, the constantly increasing demands on them by capital. Even at that the farmers seemed to be thankful for small favors, while their exploiters were getting all kinds of great favors.

The reader saw that Congressmen lost no time, but immediately acted, to give the big banks aid in 1914 to finance war profiteers to take advantage of the bargains offered as a result of the World War. On their demand Congress provided emergency currency. In 1920, 1921 and 1922 the big bankers worked their deflation scheme to force the farmers into bankruptcy and the wage workers out of jobs. Farmers and wage workers appealed to Congress for aid to save them from the attack of the profiteers but Congress, instead of aiding them, turned the job over to the big bankers.

The farmers and wage workers are still being exploited.

THE "GOOSE THAT LAID THE GOLDEN EGG"

Since writing the first chapters of THE ECONOMIC PINCH, large bankers, small bankers and a lot of big business men and politicians find that they have nearly killed the "goose that laid the golden egg"—in this case the farmer—so they are busy calling conferences and inviting the farmer to view his remains. Even Congress has been importuned to spread a little "molasses" for the farmer to lick. Therefore, I write a short chapter to caution the victims of greed to beware, lest they meet with the same sad experiences as have resulted in the past from conferences of the kind.

After intelligence had spread to the extent of making people sure that they had personal rights equal to each other, in some sections of the world, they provided certain guarantees with the idea of making use of their rights. Standing out prominently among the acts, are England's Magna Charta, 1215, and the Constitution of the United States, 1789. For a time those great documents were cited as the leading instruments of human liberty, but there was a slow economic dry rot in the business system that interfered with and deprived the people of the privileges which such acts as the Magna Charta and the Constitution were supposed to guarantee. I repeat, "slow economic dry rot." It seemed slow because we had not seen it approach, except perhaps a few of us who took pains to examine. The only slowness in fact was due to the original caution exercised by the prime movers of the system—the profiteers who, by teaching the victims to believe in the beneficence of their system, gradually got their strangle-hold to undermine human rights. The profiteers now have their own Magna Chartas and Constitutions and defy the people with theirs. They have become bold, aggressive, vindictive and merciless and command the people to support them. The process is no longer slow. It is now a swift and merciless economic war, with legal support. In spots it has taken on revolution as a counteraction. There is danger that it may do so everywhere in an attempt to solve the problems by organized butchery and other acts of madness. The unrest of Europe is an evidence of it. So it will be all over the world, unless in spots at least the people shall act in reasonable concert to establish business on a sane basis that recognizes the producer as entitled to proper reward for his product instead of remaining the victim of exploitation. The people are now robbed by legalized agencies. Relief from these conditions, so far as the United States has the power, is controlled by Congress.

Congress can make rules of action to aid the people in their relations with each other that would make a citizenship in America worth all that even our best dreams could suggest. Congress can do it, notwithstanding the Supreme Court fails to take much notice of the Preamble in the Constitution. The Preamble expresses the most far-reaching promise for justice that the human mind can comprehend, and discloses the purpose of the other sections and the purpose for which the United States became a nation. If Congressmen would read the Preamble daily, and would be true, how would it strike them in light of the Preamble to compare their acts for the profiteers with their later acts pretending to compensate the people for the profiteers' robberies, committed by authority of the earlier acts, but still leaving the earlier acts in force to rob the people of any possible advantage that the new acts might allow? Take for example the Federal Reserve Act. That law gives big bankers authority to rob the people. It has been manipulated to rob them of scores of billions in the last eight years. At the same time they have stolen the people's credit—converted it to the use of the big bankers. Now after the people are down and out by that scheme, here come the Congressmen with a pretense to atone to one group of the victims of the Federal Reserve Act—the farmers—with a batch of farm credit laws. Take the Lenroot-Anderson Act, for example. Compare it with the Federal Reserve Act and we shall see at once how Congressmen treat farmers as compared with big bankers.

Congressmen, I repeat, made the Federal Reserve Act, and Congressmen make the Lenroot-Anderson Act. The Federal Reserve Act is for the bankers, and the bankers run it for themselves. The act provides that they shall run it, and is so fixed that they could use bank deposits to seize all the gold, run to Uncle Sam with each $1,000 of gold, get $2,500 of paper money and pay only one-half of one per cent, putting up as further security paper that they get for the money that belongs to their depositors. The law forces member banks to furnish them both deposits and capital. Then they fix their own rates of interest to charge for the use of other people's money. That states only a part of the special privilege that the twelve Federal Reserve banks got from the Congressmen. Now, what do the farmers get in the Lenroot-Anderson Act? They get nothing that they do not have to *give their own security* for, and as they have been almost totally ruined beforehand by the Federal Reserve Act, their credit is not up where it should be. But whatever security they have left is what they have got to use to get new credit, and they are not allowed to go direct to Uncle Sam, like the twelve big Federal Reserve banks, and get money for one-half of one per cent. Oh, no! the farmers have *got to stack up their own security,* and for the money they borrow they will be required to pay from ten to thirteen times as much interest as the Federal Reserve banks. The farmers are forced to wait and go through a lot of red tape before they get money under the Lenroot-Anderson Law, while the Federal Reserve banks get in instantly under the Federal Reserve Act. The two acts, the Federal Reserve Act and the Lenroot-Anderson Act, are incidents in a long line of acts passed from time to time by Congressmen who have always given the profiteers practically what they asked, and never given to farmers, wage workers and legitimate business the rights that, by the laws of nature and justice, belong to them. And yet such men as these will brazenly go before the voters and claim the right to be re-elected because of such acts as the Lenroot-Anderson Law. The parasites get it all; honest industry and honest business must be grateful for a few crumbs only.

XV

THE ESCH-CUMMINS RAILWAY ACT

No extended discussion of railway laws will be attempted in this volume, nor of the much talked of Esch-Cummins Act, except to call attention to an attempt of Congressmen who voted for the act to make believe that the act does not guarantee the railways their profit. The act, to be sure, does not in expressed terms guarantee profit except for the first six months from the time the government turned the railways back to their own control, following the war. For a certain further period, it practically charged the Interstate Commerce Commission to fix freight and passenger rates to give the railways a profit, and if the profit should exceed a certain amount the excess should be divided between the government and the railways. In other words, it is something like the Federal Reserve Act; if the owners of the system should rob the people more than the law allows, the government would go into partnership, dividing the excess profits.

So far as the Esch-Cummins Railway Act is concerned, however, it must be taken in consideration with other laws to get its full meaning. Congress created the Interstate Commerce Commission. That Commission, among other duties, is charged with that of fixing freight and passenger rates to pay the railways the so-called reasonable profit. What reasonable profits are is discussed in a previous chapter. Suffice to state here that the practice is long established that 6 per cent in practice is not considered unreasonable by any tribunal that has had any hand in defining it. They are of late hewing as close to 6 per cent as they can, and if they don't make it one year they try it the next, and make it cumulative if they can. Congress itself fixed the profit of member banks in the Federal Reserve System at 6 per cent on their Federal Reserve stock, cumulative.

In the same connection we must bear in mind that the money trust is the guardian of all the other trusts. The money trust, as observed in the chapter on "Banks and the People" governs itself, having supreme authority vested in a little group of men known as the Federal Reserve Board, from whose action there is no appeal as long as the Federal Reserve Act remains in its present form. If Congress attempts to take its power away, it is likely that the question will be dragged into court on a claim that it has a vested right, and that even Congress has lost the power over the banks.

It is a fact that the profiteer group which owns the other great trusts also controls the railroads. The several trusts are operated in a way not to seriously hinder each other's profiteering. They are well agreed. Neither Congressmen nor any intelligently informed persons can dodge the fact that they themselves have knowledge of those facts, and should have them seriously in mind when they deal with legislation.

The House of Representatives has 435 members and the Senate 96. A majority of both are lawyers and bankers. Presumably they understand the English language. They also have a pretty keen knowledge of the fact that if the profiteers are given a chance to exploit the people for profit, they do it. They knew all that when they passed the Esch-Cummins Law.

The Esch-Cummins Law opens wide the door for the money trust, the steel trust, the lumber trust and all of the other trusts, when money is loaned or commodities sold to the railways, to charge robber prices; while the Interstate Commerce Commission will be expected to add the cost to the charges made for handling freight and passengers, and on top of it all add the so-called reasonable profit to be paid the railways. Or, in plain terms, the other trusts may rob their own railway trust and charge the robbery to the public in increased freight and passenger rates.

When a strike is started for some grievance it is with the idea that the strike will inconvenience the employers enough so that an adjustment may be forced. As a rule in the case of a railway strike, while the strike lasts, the strike adds materially to the cost of railway operation. During strikes the railways employ "scabs," usually inexperienced men or at the most not as efficient as the regulars; accidents increase. Accidents are expensive. Guards too are employed and various other extraordinary expenses incurred in fighting strikers. All these are charged up to the cost of maintenance and operation, on which to base charges for service to the public.

Is it any wonder that the railway officials were "cocky" against the strikers in the summer and fall of 1922? The strikers might, so far as the railway officials were concerned, resort to any excesses if they wished, for whatever it cost the railways the officials figured that it would be included in "the cost of maintenance and operation," and that the Interstate Commerce Commission would see that the railways were reimbursed in added freight and passenger rates. It is plain to see that it is one of the purposes of the act to subordinate labor, right or wrong.

XVI

"CONGRESSIONAL INVESTIGATIONS"

All such problems, as the public records disclose, have seemed to be blanks in the minds of most Congressmen when they enact laws. Nearly every important act of Congress has its glaring omissions, its failure to safeguard the rights of the people. It is unreasonable to suppose that members of such important bodies as the Senate and House—the Congress of the United States—should be so stupid as to leave the doors wide open for the profiteers to continually rob the people right and left. 'Mistakes may occur of course, but they should not be so general and always favor, or nearly always favor, the profiteers. It must be that the people are so poorly informed on what should be done by public officials, and that the profiteers are so well informed on what they want the public officials to do, that the officials take the way of least resistance and give the profiteers what they demand.

Congress is long on investigations. Whenever the people press Congress for relief from a complained-of evil—if the profiteers object—some member introduces a resolution to *investigate,* instead of Congress' taking direct action. The most frequent reason for that is to postpone action. By the time the work is completed, if ever that happens, and a report is made, other excitements in the meantime are likely to arise and the old thing be forgotten or passed over, or if that is not so the profiteers have had time to fix things so that whatever is done will still permit them to profiteer. Hundreds of millions of dollars of the people's tax payments, since our government began, have been wasted in investigations, in investigations without the slightest benefit. On the contrary, they have too often served to sidetrack needed action.

It is only now and then that an investigation of Congress serves a useful purpose. The things investigated are usually matters on which the facts are already, before the investigation starts, well known by enough members of Congress so that intelligent action could be taken. Indeed, as a whole these investigations have delayed the people in securing their rights from Congress. It is evident on every side what the trouble in our economic system is. If the members of Congress wished, they could act upon the vital problems without the delay of expensive investigations. The trouble in correcting things is that most Congressmen *dare not* take action to interfere with the profiteers.

I have had some experience with investigations. I caused the Money Trust Investigation. It developed nothing that I did not know about or that most other members of Congress did not know before I started the campaign for it. In fact, the investigators, who were mostly favorites of the money trust, did not make either a complete investigation or a complete report. If they had, it would have prevented our late panic. The proof was clear, however, that a money trust existed and that it controlled industry as well as finance. That much the report showed. It was an expensive proceeding. All the facts were clearly before the members of Congress, but still, in the face of the positive uncontradicted proof, there was not the slightest hesitation on the part of an overwhelming majority in both Senate and House in passing the Federal Reserve Act, which increased the powers of the money trust by turning over to it the absolute control of finance, including even money from the treasury of the United States.

In the early days of the World War it was evident on every side that all kinds of war-profiteering were carried on to the great loss of the people and the government, so in an attempt to stop it I urged an investigation by Congress of the actions of the war-profiteers, believing that if ever there was one time when profiteering was more dangerous and heartless to the nation than at another, it was in time of war. An investigation then would have prevented us from being so mercilessly robbed later, but the only effect my attempt had was my being charged by the profiteers, and many innocent people, with being disloyal. Later I began proceedings to head off the Federal Reserve Board in framing things for a panic after the war. Here, again, I was charged with disloyalty and action was prevented.

In both cases, if Congress had taken prompt and proper action, the nation and the people would have been saved billions that have since been lost. Now that the damage has been done there is a cry—for investigation of these cases! The only thing left to be accomplished at this late date by investigation is to remove the badges of "loyalty" worn by the rapers of the people's rights. That is desirable, but it will not save the people from the loss sustained. The current War Contract fraud prosecutions, just begun on a very small scale, are getting back a little of the people's money, and the government should get all. It remains to be seen how much will really be done. Whether war-time patrioteers or all-the-time profiteers, those who cheat nations of human beings in hours of their great need are beneath decent contempt. A noose is too good for them.

Now I have not criticised Congressional investigations because of any fundamental wrong in them, but merely because it has been the practice of Congressmen to use them as means of delay and avoidance; because many of them simply investigate what is well understood without the necessity of going to any expense of Congressional investigation.

ONE-SIDED STATEMENTS

Let any person, without information and without prejudice, go to a political meeting to hear able speakers. He thinks that he has heard the truth on the matters discussed. If it be a Republican rally he may not join the party, but he will at least agree that it is right. Let the same person next go to a Democratic rally to hear able speakers on the same subjects that were discussed by the speakers in the Republican rally, and he will be greatly surprised to find that they reason just as well as the Republicans, but come to different conclusions. He feels puzzled.

Then suppose, in his amazement, he seeks further light and goes to a rally of the Farmer-Labor party to hear equally able speakers on the same subjects. He becomes still further amazed, for these speakers present equally good reasons for their claims and arrive at still different conclusions.

If the person we have assumed had attended only one meeting, probably he would have supported the candidates of the party whose plea he heard. But having attended all the meetings and heard equally convincing talk in them all, he is bound to arrive at the conclusion that the trouble with the speakers and with himself is that the facts back of the talks have not been established by him, and possibly were not known to the speakers, and that if he is to be able to pass on the credibility of the respective speakers he must know the facts himself.

Then, having an inquiring mind and having heard three sets of speakers, each set drawing different conclusions about what our government ought to be, and still uncertain, this person scans the public press for information. Here too he becomes puzzled, for he finds that whatever paper he reads states all the good things and suppresses all the bad, if there are bad things, in the cause that it supports. He does not as a rule get an impartial discussion in either the forums of the public speakers, or in the public press.

Unfortunately, very few people take a survey of all sides, but are content to accept as true the first presentation made to them; and are forever thereafter tied to that, whether true or false. Even if perchance they later discover that a part of their first belief is false, some are so stubborn that they will not act upon the truth. Of course, that is biting off their nose to spite their face, but it is done by many. With those who are prejudiced and insist on believing without investigation of their own, there is no argument. They stand in the way of progress.

Public speakers are educators. The public press has greater influence than speakers. Both seek to make others think as they want them to act. Everyone who would know the truth is under the necessity of personal investigation, at least to the extent of enabling him to weigh the arguments of others. And personal investigation will discover all that Congressional investigators have never done.

XVII

THE RULES OF CONGRESS

It is not expected that the people will inform themselves to any great extent about the rules that govern legislative bodies. Yet certain of the rules may easily be understood and remembered, even by the least interested of us, and to some advantage, although the average member of Congress himself seldom learns all the tricks of the rules.

When the people demand action of Congress they find it very easy to get a bill introduced Any member can do that. But before the body acts on a bill, the bill must run the gauntlet of the rules. In that it meets difficulty. Both houses of Congress have made the rules to enable members to dodge responsibility if they wish. It is common for them to dodge when the public wants action to which the profiteers object, or to cover their tracks when the profiteers make demands to which the people object but which Congress grants.

The same rules that have enabled Congress to take up, consider and pass bills in the interest of the profiteers, and to strangle bills that the profiteers have opposed, can be used with equal advantage to take up, consider and pass bills in the interest of the whole people, and to strangle bills introduced for the benefit of the profiteers. It is simply a case of what Congressmen wish to do. Often a single member blocks action by the majority—an absurdity that the majority designedly imposes on itself because members are at times too cowardly to act. If Congress has the power to pass a law that a majority wishes, the majority has the power to make a rule to do it.

Of course rules are necessary, but they should not be allowed to operate absurdly with any public or private body that makes its own rules, for if it has the power to make them it also has the power to unmake them, and to make new rules.

Both Senate and House have rules that block free action by all but the leaders of the majority. The rules of the two bodies are not the same, but they have the same effect in blocking or promoting action, whichever the leaders see fit. Even the average member never learns the force of the rules, except in a limited way.

Bills and resolutions are introduced by the member drafting them, and placed in a baskét on the presiding officer's table. A clerk takes them from the basket, numbers them in the order of time, and the presiding officer should refer them to a committee. A clerk usually does that instead. The next day the bill or resolution has been put in print, a bare reference by title made to it in the *Congressional Record.* With that much done, about nineteen of every twenty bills and resolutions are pigeonholed and not followed any further in Congress, even by the member introducing. The latter obtains a few copies to send to constituents, making them believe that he is diligently at work seeking to do what they want.

If a member introduces a bill that he really means to try to pass, he must get the committee to which it is referred to give him a hearing on the bill. In the meantime, if such a request is made, the chairman of the committee examines the bill, and unless he favors it the member will have some trouble to get it even considered in committee. Comparatively few of the bills and resolutions introduced are ever considered in committee. The committee clerk files them and then they are forgotten.

When bills are at length considered by the committee, they are sure to have first been gone over by the profiteers' lobbyists. They are on guard for their clients at all times and investigate everything. If they have no objection and the committee is favorable, the committee reports the bill, with whatever recommendations it sees fit prepared by a member to whom it is referred for the purpose. Any member opposing can prepare and file a minority report. There is a way to get bills on the calendar without favorable reports from committee but it is seldom done; the bills die on the calendar in most cases.

When a bill gets on the calendar, which it does if it is favorably reported, it then meets its greatest difficulty if there is opposition, which there is certain to be if it interferes in any way with any of the specially privileged interests.

Every Congress has only two years to live. All the unfinished work at the end of a Congress, if anything further is ever done, must start again. New bills and new resolutions must be introduced and the same forms of action taken up again as if they had never previously been before Congress. Some information may be left behind by the old Congress that can be used, but for the rest it is all a matter for the succeeding Congress. That fact contains an important secret with reference to the leadership in Congress. The old members re-elected see to it that many bills either of no harm to them or to the interests they represent, or else bills that they favor, are first dropped into the basket of the new Congress, go to committees and are reported quickly to get on the calendar ahead of all others. In that way the calendar immediately becomes a blockage against the consideration of all the bills that new and less sophisticated members may be able to get reported.

The thing that happens is that the head of the calendar has always enough bills on which the leaders may manage to fritter away the time of Congress in order to prevent any bill of importance to the people being considered, if the profiteers are opposed to it and can influence the leaders to use the advantage. They usually have that influence. It also happens that these unimportant bills sometimes block the way for the consideration of bills that the profiteers wish considered. The bills must be taken up in the order of their standing on the calendar.

There are exceptions to the rule that bills must be taken up in their order on the calendar. The bill for the Federal Reserve Act, the Emergency Currency Act, the Esch-Cummins Act, and in fact almost all important acts framed for special privilege were at first far down toward the bottom of the calendar, but the leaders who framed them had no difficulty in digging them out from the bottom and getting them considered and passed.

To do such stunts there is a Rules Committee, and the Rules Committee—whenever the leaders have desired it—has been in the habit of preparing a recommendation to the main body to pass a special rule that supersedes the regular rules by bringing up the bill called for; and the time for discussion on the proposed special rule is also in the control of the Rules Committee, so its chairman alone has full opportunity to present the side for the passage of the special rule by allowing only those who favor it ample time in which to speak for it. The opponents are limited. In that way the bills that the leaders want considered are dug up from the bottom of the common mass of bills that clog the calendar, and passed. That is the way they got up for passage all the important bills in the interest of the profiteers, like those previously referred to.

As a matter of fact, the same special rule proceeding could be used to work for the welfare of legislation favorable to the people, but as long as the leaders are favorable to the special interests, and the other members are too cowardly to take matters in hand, the people's rights will stay in the background or remain buried at the bottom of the calendar, never to be reached.

Secret sessions are often resorted to to consider public matters, but are never justified except when foreign problems are involved, and only under certain conditions then. Nevertheless they are often held in order that members may shield themselves by keeping their actions secret from their constituents.

One of the practices followed to prevent the voters' knowing what the individual Congressmen do is to consider first bills that have been reported, not in the regular session of the House, but instead in a sort of committee of the whole where all members may be present and may vote without having a record made of their individual votes. In those deliberations bills are read section by section and amendments offered by any member, the members of the committee in charge being given preference, which privilege is often used to prevent other members' offering amendments. The votes are verbal. If a member questions the count he may call for a "division" which—if a certain small number of members support it—means that the votes are counted by opposing leaders, having first one side pass between them and then the other, whereupon the counters report to the presiding officer, who announces the result to the speaker without making any record of individual votes. When the House has considered a bill in that fashion the "committee" reports to the House, which is called in regular session with full powers.

In the House in regular session one-fifth of those present can demand a record vote. It often happens that many members become commited in the committee considerations in ways that they do not wish to have their constituents know, so often not one-fifth of the members will vote for a record vote. In that manner members often succeed in preventing their constituents' learning the truth as to how they vote. Even when record votes are forced, most bills have some provisions looking to the general welfare, and when those are intermingled with vicious provisions and the bill is passed or defeated, the members are still protected from information's getting to their constituents of how they voted on the detail provisions in their first deliberations; as they may explain to constituents that they voted for the bill because of the good provisions, or if they voted against it, that they did so because of the bad provisions. The constituents do not know enough about either to place the responsibility unless the bad is so bad, or the good is so good, that one of these qualities considerably overbalances the other.

Considered generally, the rules are mainly bad because the leaders, as most leaders in the past have been, were for special privilege and used the rules to accomplish the purposes of special privilege. Had the leaders, on the other hand, favored the people, the rules could have served the people equally well. Here again is where a people's organization, removed from political prejudices, can protect the public from the bad practices of the leaders who manipulate the rules in aid of the profiteers.

XVIII

THE LEGISLATIVE BLOC

The "Bloc," or "Balance of Power" as it is sometimes called, is a scheme of certain persons to group together in order to stop larger bodies from having their own way, except by compromise with the bloc. Those forming the bloc single themselves out for that purpose. The most effective bloc is formed when there are two opposing political groups, nearly equal, neither of which has votes enough to carry its purpose unless it gets votes from the bloc. The bloc, if it gets what it wants, may join either side or it may act simply as a bloc to prevent action. It is not democratic in principle, but acts more like a "dog in the manger." Therefore, an efficient bloc if selfish, and most of them are selfish—has its price. The price is usually political promotion or other favor. Laymen generally would be surprised if they knew how many public officials owe their position to some sort of original bloc scheme. All negative action has some such purpose in it, whether good or bad.

Robert M. LaFollette is making a strong effort to turn a legislative bloc to *good* purpose. The Senator from Wisconsin, in his thirty or more years of public service, has long since passed the "acid test" as a man of the common people. Any bloc led by LaFollette will be for the people! The majority who have been elected as progressives, however, after being surrounded by the special-privileged a term or two, have gone over body and soul to special privilege, or simply blown off demagogic steam and have never done anything at all constructive.

The reader must bear in mind that special privilege is in power. The laws that already exist permit, and in many cases authorize, it to exploit the people. It is well fortified in its position, if no more laws are ever passed.

For example, those who earn their living by useful work or service of any kind have experienced acute financial distress. While they have been distressed, the national and international banking groups that control finance have prospered. They prosper because they dominate the Federal Reserve banks. The Federal Reserve banks dominate the other banks. Therefore, the big bankers dominate the entire financial system. The law forces the country banks to withdraw funds from their respective communities to support the Federal Reserve banks. In that way the entire country is compelled by law and practice to finance the big bankers and finance whatever they choose to promote, while the useful people themselves are deprived. While these big bankers have been constructing palaces for their business costing millions of dollars each—the one in New York costing twice as much as the national capitol, other useful enterprises have been financially pinched. In the face of all the wrong to the people from the management of the Federal Reserve banks, not a single bill has been introduced in Congress to have the government take over the Federal Reserve banks. To stop and destroy that destructive system and adopt *government control* is now the most important of all things for Congress to do. The bloc cannot touch or deal with that problem. With the laws as they are the big bankers can bleed the common people white, which has already been done to possibly most of us. To take away that power from special privilege requires affirmative legislation. No bloc can do it. A majority of the legislators must act for the people. The bloc can be used by special privilege to prevent affirmative legislation. Special privilege may compromise and concede some things to an honest bloc, but will grant nothing that leaves it with less than it already has—unless public sentiment threaten it with danger. The people should be very wary of bloc control's becoming a general practice. In spite of hard times, in fact in the worst of times, special privilege has prospered to the very highest degree on what it already has, while the exploited people have been bedraggled in poverty and had their rights foreclosed. The fact that special privilege has had a luxurious and riotous living leads many to believe that laws may be made so the government can make a living for us all. Nothing can be farther from the truth. There is no one for the people to exploit unless they exploit the exploiters of what the exploiters have accumulated by exploiting the people. That would not last long, for in the first place most is expended in extravagance. Special privilege is not so rich in material things as it is in the continued privilege of taking toll from the earnings of the common people. With that privilege cut off special privilege would be at the end of its rope in a few weeks. It earns nothing but simply takes what others earn. It is evident to everyone who thinks and reasons on the matter that the most that can be done for the fair, honest citizen is to make laws to protect his earnings from exploitation. The government can take the privilege from the exploiters. When that is done the people will succeed.

To get anything really permanent the people must move and act with sufficient solidarity as directed by their common intelligence to impress the legislative bodies and the executives with their duties to the public. The Supreme Court also must be impressed with the duty of the court to read into the decisions for the benefit of the people the following from the Preamble to the Constitution:

"Promote the general welfare, and secure the blessings of liberty to ourselves and our posterity."

As the decisions of the Supreme Court now run, that part of the Preamble to the Constitution quoted above, which is more comprehensive than any other words in the Constitution, has in effect been applied as if it were meant not as a protection to the people, but instead to secure the general welfare and blessings of liberty for special privilege, the profiteers and their posterity.

The so-called "reasonable profit" discussed in a previous chapter, and other things in practice familiar to the reader, are amply evident of the facts stated. Special privilege has been clothed with legal privilege and in some cases with direct authority for collecting profits, in effect making industrial slaves of all humanity except the privileged few. Therefore affirmative legislation is necessary. Even if we elect to office a majority who would act in our behalf for a long time, the bloc would be used by privilege to block legislation. The so-called bloc, even in the hands of our friends in office, is futile to correct the great problems that now encumber mankind. Tariff, income and inheritance taxes, excess profits tax, super-tax, and all such are terms related only to the false system—incidents of special privilege—and reach the vital human necessities about as much as it affects a man's vitals to shave off his mustache. To strike back at special privilege in taxation is simply to enter the government into partnership with the robbers, to take from privilege a part of what it robs us, for after the government has taken it special privilege robs the government of most of it. Those collections by the government may be made as long as we follow the profiteers' game, but we must not fool ourselves into thinking that they are remedies. On the contrary, following those ideas postpones the day of a government true to the people. We are simply chopping around the edges, trying to clip off a wrong here and another there, neglecting our great fundamental necessities. The bloc is merely the "dog in the manger." When the dog is our dog it may serve us better than no dog at all, but we must have affirmative action in order to stop special privilege from jockeying men, women and children into serfdom. The bloc is no new device. It is old as civilization itself. We waste our time and our money if we put too much reliance on a bloc or on any so-called Balance of Power.

XIX

FROM LOWEST TO HIGHEST

The highest being with whom we have any personal experience is man himself. Man is foremost and we confine our thoughts to what man can do. Viewing man as he comes down the ages, two prominent distinctions are presented: Brute Force and Intellect. As between man and the other animals, man's intellect makes him master.

The lion and the tiger are forced to retreat before him, the horse and the elephant must obey. Gorillas exist but fail to develop intellect. In 1920, in Africa, a man shot a gorilla more than nine feet tall, weighing six hundred and twenty-two pounds. Perhaps no beast but the elephant could have successfully defended himself against an attack from that gorilla. The gorilla would not have had the slightest difficulty defeating one hundred men who could attack him at once, if they had no more with which to fight than the gorilla. He would have torn them to pieces as rapidly as they approached. One man with a gun killed the giant gorilla. The gun—in its make, the powder and all else—was the product of prior THOUGHT. The gorilla with only instinct and muscle—the man with muscle as nothing to that of the gorilla but acting with brain design—these two were pitted against each other. The man killed the gorilla. Without thought, man would be forced to flee, skulk and hide from the powerful beasts of prey; in fact, uncivilized tribes do that still. THOUGHT frees civilized man from fear of beasts.

When we look to the lower order of creatures upon this earth we may be proud of man. When we attempt to look into the cause of life, its endless variety and the struggles between the varieties, and when with the best telescope our vision sweeps the heavens and we see the planets that speed through space, we discover an infallible law that guides. Astronomers and others use every contrivance they can in an attempt to survey the Universe and to inquire the cause behind it. It is a study sublime, but we meet with our limit when we undertake it.

Not only are we vitally concerned with the

results of our own lives, but we must be concerned with the lives of the lower order of creatures. The microscope leads our vision into the waters, the pure and the impure, and into many substances where we find life in variety. There too we find struggle. To the unaided eye this under-life and its struggles are invisible. It goes on out of one's sight as though it were all in another world.

We ascend a trifle higher in the scale of existence to the living things seen. We find the worms, the bugs, insects innumerable, some harmless, others harmful. Those that injure us and damage anything that we want, we call harmful. They war among each other also. They live upon each other, more or less. They create disease among each other. We have specialists who observe this and inoculate the injurious insects to spread disease among them. Often in lower life it is a war between the harmful and the useful. Even bugs in this way have been brought into the service of mankind. It is not alone the ox and the horse that work for us now.

But let us come up a bit more, to the small animals, the birds, the fish. Some live upon the insects. Others make war—one species upon the other, upon several others. We find the owl by night, a robber, burglar and a murderer, attacking mice, rats, rabbits and other small animals, as well as many birds. He is a mean enemy to his prey, but it's his meat. He would perish without it. We find the hawk and the eagle pursuing boldly by day what the owl stealthily follows by night, while some hawks add fish to their menus. A hawk balances in the air, thirty feet or more above a fish resting near the surface of the water; then he swoops down, rising with the fish in his claws. The way to avoid the hawk would be to swim deeper, but cannibal fish are in the water all around, so there is no safety anywhere.

Animals all look for safety, both as to food supply and against enemies. The beaver, muskrat and several other animals make homes with water protection. Instinct may have saved them for thousands of years from the aggression of animal enemies, but instinct is often no protection against their enemy, man.

Mr. Muskrat, with his cozy house built up from the bottom of a marshy lake, extending two or three feet above the surface with inside water connections for winter use, may reconnoiter all over the lake bottom for roots, clams and fish, and return supplied. In this, one of his habits, he is safely protected against nature. But here comes a boy, walking upon clear, new-formed ice. He kicks the moss-and-grass-built muskrat house. Mr. Muskrat dives through his water connection into the lake. He swims a few hundred feet, fearful because of his recent disturbance. He is under the ice and safe from any enemy that ever before came to his notice. His lungs were full when he dove, and it's the only air under the ice at his command. He must conserve the air that is in his lungs, or lose his life. He knows. Carefully he approaches the under surface of the ice, stops a moment just below and exhales. There in the water, up against the ice, is now a bubble, holding all the air he exhaled. He is careful. His life is dependent on that bubble. He lets it rest a few seconds to purify, then glides up, puts his nose in, breathes it all into his lungs, then continues his journey. The boy has followed and watched through the clear ice. However much the boy's presence above disturbs our little animal, there is no choice for the submerged swimmer. He must continue his journey and repeat again and again the exhale and inhale of the same air. Finally the boy decides. Next time the swimmer exhales and the air bubble comes up to the ice as before, the boy with his hatchet strikes the ice. The confusion frightens the swimmer from the air bubble and he draws water instead into his lungs. The boy cuts a hole in the ice—the muskrat is his, and he later announces his discovery to the world. One more truth known!

Then there are the larger animals—the deer, elk, moose, bear, tiger, lion and dozens of others, some herbivorous and some carnivorous. Most of the carnivorous animals prowl and prey upon the others by night, the herbivorous forming their best prey. The herbivorous are not fierce defenders as a rule, though some of them have ways of defense. The elephant is large enough and strong enough to keep them all at bay. The tiger and the lion and a few of the fiercest are not much disturbed about their animal enemies. Man is their only danger, but occasionally even he falls prey to the lower animals.

Volumes could be filled with interesting facts

about the lower life creatures but only a few of their traits are stated. A boy in pursuit of a muskrat was drafted to define the difference between instinct and thought. The purpose of bringing in a few of these side incidents—the struggles between the lower creatures—is to remind the reader of what he already knows, that this is not a peaceful world.

Microbes of one kind fight microbes of other kinds, and not content with that alone they attack man and beast; insects war upon each other, as well as attack and disturb the peace of animal life; the fish eat each other; the birds are at war with each other; the animals are fighting and some fall to the others, prey for food. Man is not only fighting to defend himself against the lower creatures, but is an aggressor in a merciless war upon his fellows. *From the lowest to the highest of the living creatures there is war,* not only of the species against the other kinds, but war among themselves. Nature itself is at war with the living creatures. It refuses to support them all. If some of them were not battled down by the very laws of nature they would over-run the earth until they became their own destroyers. Caterpillars, grasshoppers and other insects and bugs multiply so rapidly that, without disease or enemies, any one of them in a few years would destroy all other living creatures by exhausting their food supply; they would even destroy themselves. Rabbits multiply with such rapidity that had they no enemies they would quickly fill the world, to be destroyed by their own multiplicity.

It is only a few years since the writer, while travelling by automobile through central Minnesota, saw thousands of rabbits. He stopped the car one evening just after sunset, and counted twenty-seven of them in the road within a range of probably forty rods. He had not seen any snakes but he had seen rabbits by the thousands! A year or so later. touring through the same country, he saw none. It was said that they had died of a contagious disease. A few survived, however, and by now they are too many for the good of the orchards and gardens.

The struggle among the lower animals we may take for granted. We have been able to domesticate a few of the species and establish fairly safe peace qualities among them. They are at least not the enemies of man. There was a time when the larger animals, especially the carnivorous, were dreaded. Among some of the lower human tribes the larger of the lower animals are still feared, but civilized man is no longer afraid of any *animal*. It is only recently that man has discovered that he has more dangerous foes in a lower order of life than he ever had from tigers, lions and other sizable animals. The deadly microbe that he cannot see attacks him unawares. But even this enemy is being discovered and plans formed to destroy it, as all the animals have been subdued, driven to run from man, or been exterminated.

We do not know beyond doubt of any place other than the earth where people live. To himself and his fellows man is accountable, because he has a mind and can reason, yet his account is unsatisfactory. We wish to find out what the matter is. We know that there is only one way to make the account balance as it should, and that is to unite mind and heart and will to do.

Our relations with each other are unreasonable. We quarrel and fight in our smaller groups, and also about things in our broader relations. We are spaced off into all kinds of districts, the larger termed states and the largest called nations. Not a nation has settled on satisfactory rules for even its people. In all of them the people complain that their personal treatment is unjust. Still, with their own affairs unsatisfactory and unsettled, they dip into the affairs of other nations, even go to war to settle disputes of less importance to the individual peoples than many unsettled hearth and home problems. Opportunities await us, at home, for wonderful achievements that would make us much more prosperous than we now are. We have been stupid in not using our best opportunities. We have been stupid in the arrangement of our industrial and business relations.

Among us are many persons who have done great things, but none have been able to put in operation a satisfactory plan for justice in industry and business. Specialists have given much service in their respective lines of work in order to know better than the average whatever work they selected, thereby giving all of us a benefit. Scientists penetrate deeply into the conditions that are mysterious to most of us, and then disclose their discoveries so we too may know. Yes, the scientists and specialists give wonderful service to the world, not only in digging out and presenting things to us, that we would not know if they did not present them for our information, but in addition making discoveries that serve us well whether we understand them or not.

Our libraries are filled with all kinds of information to give us a start in any line of action that we have time and desire to pursue. But when we think to start, we are brought up against one problem that blocks most of us. Food, raiment and shelter are at the base of our existence. Because of the difficulty to secure these, a few of us who have been lucky and not compelled to drudge for them have made progress; while the rest of us are still forced to slave for the necessaries of life.

The homes of most fathers and mothers and their personal property too are mortgaged or they have other debts, which have about the same effect on the family. The family is forced to struggle to meet the debt, or rather to pay the interest, for the principal usually runs on. The early settlers started with small debts because they could get very little credit. They paid very high rates of interest, often from two to three per cent per month in advance. The interest alone was equal to the principal in two or three years. In these later years we can borrow more, and the interest rate is very much less, but we pay more interest than was paid by the pioneers. That is because the principal is now larger. Then as now we paid all the interest we could. What we could not pay was added to the principal and repeatedly compounded to make the principal larger, so we have ever more interest to pay.

Farmers and wage workers and many small business people are not permitted to add the interest they pay to what they sell, nor to the wages if they work for wages. Speculators usually fix the prices. Farmers and wage workers are buyers of necessaries. They have very few deals directly with each other, so purchases are mostly made from the price fixers, the speculators. Unless we are price fixers we sell for what the price fixers will give, and buy for all that they ask. They say we can "refuse to sell," and we can "refuse to buy" if their prices do not suit us. Surely, we can quit work on the farm and we can refuse a job. If we do, they will arrest us as vagrants and send us to jail. In jail, other farmers and wage workers will be taxed to keep us while there. If we all quit our farms and our jobs at once there will not be enough room in the jails; besides, the fellows who send us to jail would die for want of the necessaries of life.

Unless we have more useful things than courts and jails to occupy our time we may as well go on in our same old way—work and drudge and scrimp—and let the price fixers manage. They will not actually starve us to death as long as we earn their profits for them. They make use of us as long as we are strong and can work, for them.

Visit practically any family with father and mother, boys and girls, and we shall find the important elements, there in their home, that control the world. They constitute the primary element in the development of the world. The children belong to father and mother, the mother in most cases being the important one in the early years of child development. Children manage much of the time to have their own way—that too with certain *proper limitations* is as it should be, for even with the exercise of reasonable freedom too many fail to have the necessary executive ability to make a success when they meet the serious things later in life. The more child life is dominated, the easier adults are influenced. They become accustomed to having others direct them, and do not think for themselves. That accounts for the public's giving so little resistance to political and economic wrongs.

The fights between brothers and sisters are not without their good side. Even in those they should not be checked too closely, for such conflicts give them experience to meet pugnacious, unreasonable humans that they will find in the adult world—not that their later fights include physical demonstrations, but they develop toward impositions a certain amount of resistance that they will need. When children get away from home they scrap more or less with other children—not because they belong to different families, but just because they have their little differences to settle. They have no courts to play with, as we adults have, so the simplest way is to fight it out. They would not seem like children were that not so. It would be sad indeed had we all been born grown-ups, so there are no regrets.

Yet the spicy conflicts between children are not so outstanding as the great pleasures, uncountable pleasures, that all the healthy have in their sports with each other. Intermingling fights with fun is mostly fun. Children are not all play, but they are all energy, and are very serious a part of their time. Children think better, harder and more seriously than is generally supposed. That is especially true of those whose parents are poor, who cannot give their children all that they consider they should properly have. When children of poor parents meet children with plenty, it sets the poor to thinking and they discuss the matter with their parents. The parents ponder it. It forms a sad drama of life, a tragedy that is experienced by the majority.

None of us has grown up in a day, but as the things of the world go trooping by we see these things. We must look back, and look ahead, and look all ways and think, if we would understand the world.

Our earliest recollections place us as little boys and girls. We then belong to father and mother. We do not doubt their ownership, but their management of us we often question. Somehow we manage more or less to have our own way, if it does not materially conflict with what the parents think ought to be. At first we are not troubled to go to school. That is no regret to the boy, ordinarily, because it is more interesting to a boy to select his own fun. He would rather take to the river, the lakes, the woods or whatever it is that exists in nature where he grows up. When it first comes time for the boy to go to school he does not take his mind there with him. He is ordered to go and he goes, but his mind goes back to where his sports have been. If one can't take his mind with him to school, school is a decidedly uninteresting place. There is a little difference between boys and girls about the first years of school. The girls adapt themselves to school earlier, and show better progress. My sympathy is with the boys of tender years, while my admiration goes to the girls.

Our schools are very good, in many respects. We pay dearly for them, more dearly than our fathers and mothers did for our schools, so the children of today are better educated than we were. Fifty years ago children spent one quarter the time in school that they do now. The girls especially are better educated, for they are considered more important now than they were a generation back. The girls in the years long ago were just as important as they are now, but the world had the fool idea then that it was not as important to educate the girls as it was to educate the boys. The majority of us have come to our senses, and those who have not will have to take the consequence, for from now on we all vote, and the schools to prepare us will give to boys and girls equal opportunity. Even if girls were not so educated in the time long past, those who were boys and girls then came on together through the intervening period between then and now, getting much the same experiences, with the result that women are as competent as men.

While a college education has its advantages, it is not indispensable to sound thinking. A true observer in the trials of life knows the everyday things of the world and need not be fooled merely for the lack of a diploma to hang on the wall. Schools and colleges now could work a little closer to nature than they do, to the advantage of both boys and girls, men and women, not only for their health, but to give them more interest and more executive force.

The masses of humanity lack in executive ability and are beaten in the game of life as it is now played, largely because of that lack. Some of the truths of nature that it is important to know, in order to judge correctly and make adult life more practical, are suppressed. Several historical works are now being excluded from our schools, not because of errors in the contents of the books themselves, but because it is the purpose of certain interests to mold opinion to endorse the purposes of those certain interests, whether right or wrong. If the teachers dare to express the truth in opposition to those interests, their jobs are always taken from them.

Teachers are no longer independent in teaching everything that many of them justly believe should be taught. Just what the influence is that seals the mouths of teachers—though it does not stop their thinking—and prevents student youth from getting certain facts that it properly should have, it is not necessary to discuss here.

Give children the facts and they will correct things when it comes their time. But before that we shall see worse times than we have now unless we parents learn the truth, teach it at home and force it to be taught in the schools. The children are entitled to information both at home and in the schools.

XX

ECONOMIC EVIL, AND "PROGRESSIVES"

Those who now dominate all things have no right, moral or fundamental, so to rule and exploit us. It is a matter of expediency, they think, for them to do it just as long as *we* have not sufficient knowledge to run things. Who of us dares honestly to blame them, so long as we know no remedy? Leaving things as they are, who among us would not use the advantage if he could take it? Some of us might wish to do better, but the majority are human.

If all the wealth that these exploiters have taken from us should today be turned back *pro rata* to the persons who earned it, or to their successors in toil, and our laws and the construction and application of our laws remained the same, everything would quickly go back to the present conditions. Those who now have the might, believe it very expedient for them to keep it. The faultfinders with nothing to offer are not over half-baked, and if given power would do no better.

Practically every person who was ever elected to office for the first time ran against someone in power who was charged with being reactionary, but who himself was originally elected as a progressive to knock out someone preceeding him who was also charged with being reactionary, but had originally been elected as a progressive; and so on we might follow back to the beginning of time. The progressives resort to too much personality in telling of wrongs done. If we could escape from these wrong-doers a lot of good might come to us by having them pointed out, but they hold us fast, not so much because of themselves as because the laws and practices permit them to. It is not so important to us to know who robs us if we are really to be robbed, as it is to know how to stop that robbery for all time.

As citizens we may favor heavier taxation of the profits of the profiteers as long as we are governed by a robber system. It should be understood however that such taxation is no remedy for economic wrongs. It does seem strange that the government should acknowledge the right of a robber system to exist, and offer as the only remedy a system for the government to rob the robbers of a little part of what the robbers rob us, the people. There are already laws on our statute books by which the government goes into partnership on excess profits. The Esch-Cummins Railway Act and the Federal Reserve Bank Act are both examples of a government entering into partnership on excess profit. Some day laws will be made what they should, and the people who make them right will look back on us with a good deal of curiosity because of our pathetic gullibility.

One progressive (?) tells us, for example, that we must levy a ten cents a ton tax on iron ore that the steel trusts take out of the earth. He says we will not have to pay so much tax on our homes then. If we have homes in Minnesota that would give us not only a direct benefit, but also an indirect loss that might overbalance our benefit. That is, the steel trusts, in accordance with the laws of trade, would add the ten cents to the price of their steel products, for the railways and other buyers to pay. Then we would repay the steel trusts—plus extra expense to them in increased freight rates and the higher price on steel goods. Yes, Minnesotans might get a direct advantage, but our brothers and sisters in other states might break even with us by a levy on some other trusts. It's alright to tax anybody, but let us not fool ourselves into believing that to do so is necessarily a remedy for our economic ailments.

Another progressive (?) says, "Let's fix a minimum wage." As was noted in a former chapter, whatever the wage the price fixers will see to it that the wage is included in the product—plus—and that the buyer of the product must pay, so while the worker gets a direct benefit, that direct benefit may be overbalanced on things that he buys. It is not wrong to fix a minimum wage, but let us not be fooled into believing that it will settle economic wrongs.

Here comes one more progressive, (?) who tells us we must find foreign markets for our surplus products, whether we need any products that the foreigners have to sell us or not, and this same progressive cries from the housetops that we must conserve our American resources. It never occurs to him that we waste our resources if we export them to foreign markets, unless the foreign markets have something more than cash to offer us. They must have goods of some kind that we need with which to pay us or to tender in exchange. Of course money may be used as a matter of convenience to facilitate exchange, but a mere money consideration is economic farce. For a mere money proposition it is to our disadvantage to export things that are useful to us.

If we had an honest money system our trade relations would be honest. For example, we exported so much petroleum 1913 to 1919 that it reduced our home supply, which gave the oil and gas trusts their excuse to raise the price on petroleum and gas to American consumers. American consumers paid, in additional price alone, more than the entire export lot brought in the foreign markets, including cost of transportation, commissions and all else.*

*For a given twelve months in 1915 and 1916, domestic consumption of petroleum was 211,933,000 barrels.

In addition to supplying that, the oil trusts exported 55,466, 088 barrels.

Formerly we bought gas for less than 12c. a gallon, but after the trusts exported millions of barrels to foreign markets, suddenly the price for us was doubled. Still they tell us that that shows a "favorable balance of trade" for America. They, and we, come about that near the truth (?) in our statements as to many

Prior to the export demand the price was 75c. per barrel for western products and $1.54 for the eastern products.

With the demand for export, however, the Oil Trusts made an excuse to raise the price on the western oils to $1.55 and the eastern to $2.60, an increase of 80c. and $1.06 respectively.

About one-fifth of the home consumption was of the eastern product, four-fifths of the western.

That manipulation cost the American consumers for twelve months alone $180,000,000 over what they had to pay before the export began, a sum far in excess of all that the Oil Trusts realized out of the 55,466,088 barrels exported.

The loss to American consumers on petroleum for a single 12-month period is a mere bagatelle compared with what it amounts to in a period of years.

The American supply of petroleum is forever reduced and the American consumer will always have to pay more than he would if we had true conservation. Petroleum is only one item. This is a concrete example of the way the system works.

economic problems. Is it any wonder that the Standard Oil Co. of New Jersey paid its 400 per cent dividend in 1922, and that another of the Standard Oil companies paid 900 per cent?

Lest it be overlooked, attention is called to the fact that the big bankers too have a "progressive" (?) idea. Instead of our financial resources' being used to protect American home industry, great bankers make foreign loans for speculative purposes, while the farmers, wage workers and small business men in our own country are driven to the wall for lack of money. Like the doubling and trebling of the price of universally needed gas by the oil trusts, because of monopoly and export, the big bankers because of the export of money increase the interest charge to native American borrowers. The total interest collected on foreign loans equals only a small per cent of increased interest charged to American borrowers.

Numberless other one-idea progressives (?) could be cited to prove that their progressive ideas in most cases are annulled by inconsistencies similar to those described. And that is why most of the political progressives are progressive enough to last for only one or two elections—long enough to defeat former so-called progressives who merged with the reactionaries quickly and quite naturally after they had been elected. Most of the so-called progressives are not progressive at all. They are simply opportunists. They do not reason to determine what inevitably will result from certain conditions. On the contrary they wait till they see the result, and are therefore trailers instead of progressives.

The true progressive is constructive. In advance he takes into consideration everything that bears upon the future, and determines from the facts what known conditions, if allowed to continue, will produce. Therefore he knows in advance the result of any political or economic policy followed, and shows publicly what is necessary to secure favorable conditions and how to avoid the unfavorable. Many of the so-called progressive Congressmen, for instance, have never been progressive. If they vote against a bill that slightly favors the profiteers, or if they criticise it or criticise the profiteers, they deem themselves constructively progressive. The only reason that there is need for *true* progressives is because many laws, practices and conditions that now exist are not what they should be. The bad laws must be repealed or amended, if amendment can make them right; new laws when necessary must be passed and bad practices be superseded by proper action.

As things are now the pains outweigh the pleasures of life for most of us, simply because most of us do not take the time to think and act upon well-formed thoughts. It reminds us of the persons described in "Main Street."* The people of Main Street in politics and economics are infinitely more ludicrous and ridiculous than the people of Main Street in "Gopher Prairie." But if we are to laugh about it it should be a pathetic laugh, for "Gospher Prai-

*"Main Street," it is sufficient to state, is a popular book. Its leading portrayal amounts to ridicule of certain country folk for their idle gossip, thoughtless mannerisms, in which they are made to appear so innocent in comparison with highly sophisticated and supposedly better-informed city folk, that their very innocence makes them frivolous and ridiculous. "Gopher Prairie" is the name the story gives to a town where these things are supposed to occur, but it is intended by the author, so most readers think, to represent a condition in all small towns.

rie'' in politics and economics is typical of every city as well as village, and all the country besides, the whole world over. It's all Main Street, in which a majority of people are so careless of their own political and economic rights that they stupidly allow themselves to be governed by laws and practices that turn the good things that properly belong to the people over to a few individuals. If any of the people were to attempt to call at the front door of the mansions of those specially favored by our laws and practices, they would be spit upon and sent to the back door to state their errand to the servants.

No! We cannot laugh at such stupidity on the part of so many, for all the poverty, most of the crimes, the wars and other woes of humanity are due to the Main Street citizens who go trooping to the poles, casting their votes, not knowing that they vote against their own best interests. Voters must know the principles involved in honest business supported by honest politics. As long as they do not know, the few who benefit from the voters' ignorance will lead the campaigns to have them register and vote. When the voters know the truth, they will register for themselves and vote too. No business is more important.

An unfortunate circumstance of the whole thing is that when a majority refuses or fails to take the time to think right and to act right in these affairs, it forces those who do think and act right to suffer the same political and economic wrongs that the careless and thoughtless impose upon themselves by their failure. We exist as a great community with interests in common, except the comparatively few who by an adroit system are able to utilize the industry of the rest of us to their own advantage and always without a return service. These few are the exception, for as long as we support them in an extravagance that is impossible to the rest of us they are really outside of the general rule.

Even when the voters happen to elect a true statesman to high office, if he is not rich enough to employ sufficient, competent help he cannot put forth his best efforts. There are so many ordinary individual demands, important to the person but of comparatively little consequence to the public, that these lesser demands take too much of the statesman's time. He is unable to work out to perfection the more important demands of the public when all these smaller things take up his time. Then, too, he is in demand to speak to his constituents. While he usually enjoys doing so, nevertheless it, too, is a draft upon his time that seriously interferes with constructive work which is much more needed. Should he fail to respond to the less important demands and put all his energy to the more important, as things are now politically, his constituents would not understand it and would defeat him at the first opportunity.

XXI

GOVERNMENT; NATION; PEOPLE

There is a difference between the government of the nation, and the nation itself.

Our country is our nation. The people of the nation are included. The government, as the word "government" is used in the discussion, is the administration of the political and industrial affairs of the people. As a people we stand for the nation when we support the common welfare. The true citizen and the true statesman do so under all circumstances. For that very reason the citizen may deplore the administration of political and industrial affairs and criticise both the government and the laws, but he is in duty bound to obey both. When any law or the government is wrong, it is nevertheless to be obeyed till by proper proceeding the wrongs can be remedied. That is the way every honest and intelligent citizen must feel when he examines carefully the way things are run. The citizen is not true to his country unless he criticises and shows wherein the government is wrong, so far as he knows, and does his best to improve things.

Owing to industrial wrongs, some sanctioned by law, our country stands in danger. To save the nation we are forced at once to criticise its government and to work to better things. It would be folly to criticise if criticism were not followed by attempts for corrections. We have reached a stage where we must make our votes count, not necessarily so much in the election of our choice of candidates—though that is desirable if we use good judgment—but our votes must count in the intelligence of knowing what should be done by whoever may be elected. Our knowledge of our rights must be so complete that for any set of officials to deny political action to meet properly the necessities, whatever they may be, would be inexpedient for the officials, even when demagogues. If we present in concrete form those things which are necessary to the people, and the people themselves know why they are necessary, no filibustering public officials will dare show their heads in opposition.

Election after election we have gone on voting, blind as bats in the sunshine, blind to what was necessary to the general welfare. Light dazzles the bat. Falsehoods have dazzled us. We have believed the false to be true, the true to be false, in too many cases. Falsehoods have too often controlled us. The falsehoods have dazzled us as light dazzles the bat, only we lack the instinct of the bat to get away from what confuses. Facts multiply so rapidly, the false and the true commingled, that we fail to sort out the truth from the great, confused mass. We require light, the light of intelligence to direct us, in order that we may act together. We have been driven by propaganda into the face of complications that we have failed to understand, and have been fooled and cheated on every turn. There is no cure for the bat's not seeing in the sunshine. Its eyes are not suited to see in bright light.

There is a cure for our confusion if we get the facts before us in the right way. Our MIND was made to use at all times. We must analyze the facts into simple, everyday truths, then sort the true from the false, and we shall not be confused. All of us should think. Somebody must think on all these troublesome problems, and unravel the tangle to make things right.

We have daily necessities. They are food, water, wearing apparel, places to live, education, recreation and entertainment. They are easily obtained if we go at it right. We struggle hard enough for advantages, but not in the right way to get them.

The province of the worker is all things. Some must produce food and the stuffs from which foods are prepared. Others must produce wearing apparel and provide the materials for their make. Others again must produce the material required to build and keep in repair our homes and places of business. Still others must aid us with our education and fit us to entertain and be entertained, in order to live wisely and well. Exchanges in everything are required, to sell what we have that we do not want, and buy what we want that we do not have. What we have to sell must be moved to where it is to be used, and what we buy must be brought to us. To accomplish all such things and make them effective is the province of the workers—the farmer, the wage worker, the men and women engaged in useful business, and all others who serve needs.

Whoever works faithfully to make it easy for us to have right advantages, occupies a useful place in life. All the advantages that exist or that can reasonably be secured belong to the useful workers, whatever their work. They are entitled to them when they serve. Every agency that encumbers the usefully occupied in securing their rights must be removed. All the able-bodied must be made to earn what they consume—to give service for service.

Everyone consumes and we must have production for the purpose. Some of us are extravagant consumers, while most of us have not enough. What we consume must be produced. The workers are the producers. Unjustly, we are not all workers. Whoever consumes without producing or giving service, or consumes more than he produces or returns in service, causes others to work that much more for that much less. Certain practices force the workers to have the least advantages for themselves. The workers alone can make the change which will make them first in the enjoyment of the good fruits of their labor.

Men and women are arbitrarily classified with reference to their wealth, social standing, their work, their advantages and disadvantages. The so-called "upper class" are least in number —mostly the rich non-workers and big spenders. Comparatively few of them do useful work. The few who do are generally extravagantly paid.

Those who form the so-called "upper class" are parasites. Parasites consume what others produce and reduce the producers' advantage to that extent.

World over, the useful working classes are objecting to the injustice of the non-workers and the uselessly employed having the most advantages. Both our own country and Europe are suffering serious difficulties because of dissatisfaction with the existing order of things. For the non-workers and the uselessly non-occupied to live in extravagance, while the usefully occupied workers live in comparative poverty, will cause trouble with all self-respecting peoples.

That a change will come—and come before long—no one with an eye to actual conditions doubts. That change will be orderly, or chaotic, according to the way we use or fail to use our heads.

The problems with which we have to deal are:

(a) Finance, now managed by bankers for profit.

(b) Transportation, incorporated and dominated by big bankers for profit.

(c) Coal, oil, iron and other minerals, timber, water-powers, all owned by trusts dominated by big bankers.

(d) Packing and storage agencies, mainly controlled by trusts dominated by big bankers.

(e) The private press—erroneously called the public press—owned and controlled mostly by excess-profit men, and used to deceive voters and cause them to elect to office politicians who serve the profiteers.

(f) Politics, dominated by the same influence as that above described.

There are other factors, but those stated are the main influences employed for exploitation by the profit men. It is these agencies that create the so-called "classes." When we deal wisely and sanely with these iniquitous agencies there will be no serious trouble.

The scheme of controlling us is very clever. The press is used to fool enough of us to give the interests the balance of power. Press falsehoods have been taken too long by too many of us as gospel truth. Our lessons are experience. The press editorials, and the material that has been run as news items the last eight years and especially emphasized would seem like a joke if we did not realize the dire consequences of our having believed the falsehoods.

We know that there is an immediate change due—not for a new and different set of falsehoods and propaganda to fool us to remain in the same old rut, though we know that will be attempted but a change that will be a determination on the part of the people to secure political and economic justice. What now rankles the voter, since he begins to see for himself instead of following blindly in the trail of false leaders, is the fool that he has been in the past, serving profit men by his votes. It is his business now to consider the key factors.

In this age of thought, man has created problems of his own making—mighty problems—problems of how to escape from his own errors and wrongs. Divided into opposing groups, man is his own enemy. His problems today are to master his own false ways. He blocks his own progress. His greatest problem is how to master himself. Here again is demand for deeper and better thought than before. It is no longer a war of beast against man. It has become a war of men against each other. Intellect is battling with intellect—not so much in thought where it concerns politics and business to discover truth, as in tricks to evade and to conceal truth when that serves the evaders best—all for what? It is done to control politics and monopolize wealth.

Huge wealth is stored in the bowels of the earth as well as upon its surface. The labor and genius of mankind are gathering it for use. For the possession of this wealth there is continuous strife. To get it from the earth and then to possess it men have organized industry. Organization has been along lines that make monopoly certain—more, it is already accomplished. By force of circumstances monopoly drafts men and women into its service to create wealth for monopoly. Mankind is now subject to the prey of monopoly, as primitive man was subject to the prey of fierce animals.

Monopolists have intellect and they employ their intellect to prey upon the industry of men, women and children. Greater intellect therefore is required to master monopoly. Intellect bids men and women to be free from the prejudices of their own past, and to look to the simple natural laws to guide them. Mr. and Mrs. Voter are face to face with it all. Their sober honest thinking must rise above the scheming intellect of monopolists—and make way for justice to rule. As soon as men and women free themselves from the cunning of monopolists, and instead follow the natural law for a fundamental basis in the management of things, they will be free. Monopoly will then serve instead of enslave, as it does now.

XXII

THE WAY OUT

In the foregoing sections I have attempted to deal with abstract subjects and concrete acts in a human way. There is no need to say why. The reader will naturally draw his own conclusions and should. In fact, individual action is needed rather than a "following." If we can have individual action, based on truth, we will come to pretty much the same conclusion, and if that individual action becomes general we shall have a successful people—otherwise not.

The hardships of the world are due mostly to the masses' following leaders and not all having minds of their own. Blind following of leaders is pitiful. It destroys the noble purposes for which mankind must have been created. It is ambitious leadership and blind following that is really the trouble with us. Leaders are like petted and pampered children—spoiled and no good unless by our intelligence we force them to be good. A great leader leads the best, when the people know what the best is.

In every human brain are the cells required to develop intelligence of very high order. In most human minds these are not developed to the degree that frees the person from prejudices, so we live prejudiced and we die prejudiced; and we have lost. We die without understanding much about the world. Such waste of good, sound brains to build from is the blight of humanity and the throwing away of happiness. With the examples of chaos, increasing wrongs, and the spread of poverty our eyes begin to open, our brains to work. The prospect is that we shall yet save humanity from destroying itself.

The greatest of the human powers lie dormant in the brain. We could get infinitely more good out of life by waking our sleeping brain cells than we experience in following the common way. Should we suddenly dispense with our prejudices and take a look at ourselves and at others in the bright light of our world as it is, in the face of the evident facts, what would our judgment be?

Answering the question, we should find ourselves small whereas we might have been great, but our company would be legion, and since it is said "misery likes company" we should not be lonesome. And there is a beacon light at the end of every consideration, for we know that within us exist latent powers which, if we put them to use, will give us the capacity to deal aright with each other; it is only a question of our using those powers!

It may seem discouraging to look back over the history pages of six thousand years, yet what use to think of it in that light when the new way lies ahead. It is within the lives of some still living that the power of steam has been developed to its present effectiveness in service. Photography has gone to work with new intelligence to impart. The human family has taken to commercial and pleasure flying—giving us a qualityof birds in the air. Electricity is rapidly being applied to almost all uses, and makes the world's doings come to the mental vision like a flash. New numberless other important developments have taken place within the memory of persons living, and in a short time all or most of these great advances may be excelled by achievements still greater. Who knows?

Practically the only thing clearly in sight and known to be a need that is in our power to accomplish, and that we have failed in, is a way to deal with each other so that the wonderful discoveries of good and useful things that can serve shall be available to *all of us.* The greatest of the world's problems is how to clear the way. All that has been gained should be applied to that one high purpose. It is by no means impossible, nor even improbable, that it will be accomplished to the advantage of us now living. There is every reason why we should secure the great advantage soon, if we act upon our opportunities.

The beacon of light is before us, for in every conscious existence—whether individual or aggregate—there comes a time when false prophets and corrupt leaders can no longer determine action. That time will be when we see their errors instead of letting them point to others' faults, as has been their habit in the past. It will be when we begin to determine for ourselves, when we take the responsibility in order to be right. We must create our conditions and not let other people create the conditions that control us to our disadvantage. We must use our own power to create the relations we may properly choose with each other and with the world.

THE ECONOMIC PINCH

BOOK II

I

THE GREATEST GAME

General political and economic conditions of the country have been carefully covered in Book I. In Book II we shall take up only those rules and moves which I believe, after much study, will enable the workers—including legitimate business in the term—to improve their ways of business and living, and come nearer to those rights of the individual as foreseen by our forefathers when they wrote the Constitution.

The struggles of humanity in business and for the advantages of life are not realized by many of us to be a game. Let us think of it as a game, for that is what it is when we take into consideration the way the capitalists treat it; and we shall name our game "Capital and Labor."

If we looked upon our business affairs as a game and ourselves as players, we should play better, without so much hard feeling, and we should also be more sportsmanlike, learn the tricks of the play and have the satisfaction of being on the winning side. We all know we have the best equipment, for the laborers outnumber the capitalists, and are right. We have not heretofore known the fine points of the game and so we have always lost. It is not our lack of interest in sport. Our intense interest in sports has been demonstrated to me on numerous occasions.

In 1921, I had the opportunity to watch a New York crowd at Times Square, during the issuing of the bulletins on the Carpentier-Dempsey bout. I was in a building where I could look down upon those thousands of people, impressed with the intense excitement they were experiencing. Every few seconds a bulletin would appear, and with each bulletin the air was filled with deafening cheers for the winner. It was evident that friends of both were in that mob. After watching from a distance I decided to learn more by going into it. I found them all talking about the big fight that was on.

Everywhere it was the same: whether for one contestant or the other, there was nothing else of importance at that time but the contest that was being played between two muscled, well-trained men. Thousands of rich and poor had paid dearly for the privilege of being at the scene of the fight, some having come hundreds and even thousands of miles for no other purpose, and those who saw the contest were even more intensely excited than the crowds that were gathered in all parts of the world to wait for reports. The actual fight did not last long, but when it was over and the last bulletin had appeared the rush for the press began. Hundreds of newsboys sold their papers to these people, who seemed to want every scrap of information on the fight. So important was this matter to them that to avoid losing any item, they bought a copy of every newspaper.

Well, what about all that excitement? It was over two men, muscled from ear to toe more than the average, and trained to fight with a science. They entered the ring to determine the world championship, and for that one must pound the other to insensibility for at least ten seconds, or the contest would be decided on points. Just that caused this intense excitement over almost an entire world.

It would be interesting to know what progress would be made toward securing industrial and political justice if we took as much interest in *the game of life* as we do over a prize fight or any of the other popular games. When compared with the game of life—capital against labor—what a travesty the excitement of the people over that ring fight appears! While the prize fight between the champion and the contestant for the belt causes the greatest excitement, it is by no means the greatest game played. The game of capital against labor is the greatest of them all. It is not staged, or styled, by the press as a game. But it is as adroitly maneuvered as a game, and has more fine points to win or lose than any other. To know the game and to play it right decides between failure and success in life itself.

Most of us have not played this game right, so the capitalists have always won and the workers have always lost. We should look for the scraps of information as eagerly as the fight fans looked for the information on the Carpentier-Dempsey contest; and then we would see the contest of capital against labor, and we would be in on the stakes too.

The stake for which the game of capital against labor is played is capital itself. Capital carries with it mansions, many servants, the most expensive cars, travel in luxury, extravagances of all kinds that suit the fancy, and an estate for their children greater than that with which the capitalists themselves started. Those things are the winnings of the game, winnings paid for by the losers.

The losers have only ordinary or poor houses, generally rented; they have no servants; if they have cars, which most of them have not, they are of the cheap and less comfortable makes; if they travel, which most of them cannot afford, they can have no luxury; they cannot indulge in general extravagances, whatever their fancy; they have the sorrow of seeing their children join the army of workers before their education is near completion; they have no estates of value to leave to their children or for any purpose. They live mostly from hand to mouth, because they have lost the game.

The capitalists line up to represent capital

and the workers line up to represent labor. The capitalists are the profiteers and speculators of various types, swivel-chair operators, gamblers — a miscellaneous assortment of schemers who seek to get and spend wealth that they have not earned or ever given service for. Labor includes all those who are engaged in the production and exchange of foods and wearing apparel, and those providing for the conveniences and necessaries of life, of whatever kind. We know the latter as farmers, wage workers, useful business operators, educators—everybody in fact that gives a service.

The contest centers on the ownership of property: the profiteers on one side seek to keep what they already have, adding what more they can, while labor on the other side—without income property to start with—seeks to gain capital by keeping the surplus of its own earnings. Of the fine points, the principal one is for the capitalists to confuse the workers, and split them into different camps fighting among themselves over matters of no importance to the capitalists, while capital goes on with its game of exploiting them all.

But politics control the rules of this game.

That makes politics important, for as the rules go so goes the game. It is not a clean sport, and if baseball were played like it, it would be abolished by the public. Those who make these rules are selfish and make the rules in their own favor; the other side cannot win; "the dice are loaded." That is exactly what has happened in the game of capital against labor. The capitalists have controlled politics and have always made the rules of the game; they have also always done their own refereeing.

Politics have been controlled by a trick. The decoy has been to hold up beautiful and true principles for honest action and consequent good-will among men. The same ideals, practically, are stated in different form, and make the excuse for political parties. With parties formed, some of the players in the game on the side of capital, become candidates for public office in each of the parties, and preach the beautiful ideals and purposes of the party to which they belong, at the same time exposing the tricks of the candidates of the other parties. Whichever candidates the voters flock to in the greatest numbers, win, but that does not mean that the party wins or the voters win.

When the election is over the capitalists *control.* They do not have to consider party principles in running the game, for after the original good deeds of a party have once won the voters' favor, those original, now hollow virtues are paraded and win again and again. A few of the leaders form inner circles, controlling those of their own gang on the outside by the bribes of patronage, committee places or other favors. Thus the machine is built. The game is won.

The rank and file of the people—the workers—are on the outside with no knowledge of what goes on inside, except that *they* have the costs and expenses of the thousands of different schemes to pay in taxes. The capitalists play bolder and bolder until a lot of workers who ordinarily play into their hands, every now and then get disgusted, join with the workers who have stood by their own game, and together elect a few who have taken advantage of the discord to exploit themselves and thus are called progressives. Progressives usually rise on the tide of dissatisfaction, but many of them have no constructive ability behind them. Besides, there are never enough elected at one time to have much influence in the building of government.

Instead of getting excited over individuals who seek to build themselves up through our excitement over their game, let us have excitement over our own game, understanding the very things that control us. Then it will not matter who happens to hold office: our general knowledge of the game and of our rights will compel the game to be played as it should be. We have become glad many times within the memory of most of us now living, when we have kicked out a few of what we called the old reactionaries, stand-patters, and put progressives in their place. But we have not progressed economically, industrially, or politically. In all three we are worse off now than ever before.

Had it not been for a few geniuses in science, mechanics and in all fields of service except economics and politics, the profiteer system would have reduced the majority of us to mere beasts. The world has made wonderful progress in everything—except politics and economics. And failure in the latter is due to our own ignorance of how to play the game. We know what we want, but we don't know how to get it. If here and there are some who do know, others of us stand in their way. We block them in everything they undertake in our favor, for the profiteer capitalists fool us to play the game into their hands.

Back a few years, we had the Populists, seeking to give the farmer his rights, but they had neither the wage worker nor legitimate business to help them. The capitalists won, as they always have. Later came the Bull Moosers, but they did not have with them the progressive rank and file of the voters who had supported both the old political parties. Capital won. It matters not what the purpose of the Bull Moosers was, they could not win. Later still we had the Non-partisans, championing mainly farmers' rights, but they did not have enough support from the wage workers and scarcely any from business. So capital-kept them from securing the farmers' rights. They are still fighting desperately for these rights, but cannot win alone.

Other moves on the part of dissatisfied groups could be cited, but it is unnecessary to name them all to show to anybody interested that isolated, single-handed attempts on the part of one group, to correct economic evils, will always in turn be defeated. The sop of victory for a few candidates often postpones any real work on the part of the people for themselves, because they expect those whom they happen to elect to do it all. Soon they see that most of those elected take the course of least resistance and do nothing. Then the people begin to think of a future election, to be lost again in the same way. So it will go until the people begin to figure out their own problems.

The sum and substance of the whole is that we, as a civilized people, have enormous requirements that entail a vast variety of demands upon the human family for all kinds of service, involving all kinds of work; that we are in absolute need of each other, and must come at once to an understanding of our respective rights and of how to secure them, to repel the stranglehold that capital successfully fastens upon us.

II

TEAM-WORK FOR VICTORY

The farmer, the wage worker and the legitimate business enterprises must stand together as a united force, not to be separated for separate defeat by capital. In order to stand together the relative rights of the farmer, the wage worker and legitimate business must determine their respective claims. Even though they cannot be made to square perfectly, they can and will be made infinitely better-fitting than at present. All three groups will thereby become independent of the capitalist or profiteer. The capitalist who is not profiteering is not the subject of this discussion.

Organization is required to include all useful groups. That organization must have a forum in which each group can first work out its own problems, independent of the other groups. As soon as these problems are worked out they must be submitted to the organization, so that all the groups may together adjust their differences. They can all yield much to each other, because the difference between what they singly get now, and what the capitalist profiteers wrongfully take from all of them, is so great that each could forego what is required and still be gainer. When the adjustment has once been agreed upon, they must unite when necessary to get whatever political action is necessary. When done in that way there will be no politicians remaining on the capital side. The game will be won, and after that every industrious person will find it easy to prosper; the way to contentment and good-will will be cleared. In any undertaking those who expect to get the benefit must not only know the purpose, but must have a knowledge of everything connected. In the game of politics the rank and file of voters do not know enough about it to get any advantage anywhere. The advantage goes entirely to the leaders who betray them. The voters have not had sufficient knowledge of politics to know all their advantages if the game were played honorably.

To get that knowledge suggests a more complete organization. At first a people's organization would not have all the advantages of the newspapers' help, for the press is under the domination of the profiteer capitalists, not so much by choice as by forced condition. Supported by the capitalist profiteers the press meets the obligations of its own expenses. The public in turn is exploited.

As noted in Book I, the United States Chamber of Commerce, an organization supported by the capitalists, is fashioned very much on the order suggested here, only that organization is on the other side of the game. The capitalist profiteers dominate it.

In addition to literature to circulate among the membership of the organization here proposed, the people should meet in their respective localities to consider problems of interest. The exchange of ideas in such gatherings, and the discussion that would arise out of consideration of the literature published, would be of immense influence. It would take only a short time for the people to become familiar with the things that take place in the country. It would be impossible for Congress and state legislative bodies to enact laws that would receive the praise of the capitalistic press for years, with only the actual administration of the law itself as the first notice to the people that it operates against and not for them. That condition was exemplified in very positive and disastrous consequences in the case of the Federal Reserve Act, again in the Esch-Cummins Act. Both clearly showed upon their faces that they could be used by the profiteer capitalists as further means to exploit the people for billions of dollars. Of course the capitalist profiteers would do it when they had the chance. They would not be human if they did not, nor profiteers.

While there is much to complain of in the way politics and business are operated, not all things are bad. There is much that is good, and the conditions for making all things good are favorable provided we, the people, do the part that we are by the very nature of things supposed to do. We are not dumb beasts intended to leave our affairs entirely in the hands of a few super-men and super-women, whether right or wrong. Even if our political and industrial leaders were statesmen and business men and women of the very highest order, were absolutely unselfish and would pilot the game wholly for us and give us all the advantages that could be given, still we should need to know how things were run. There is no excuse for our ignorance on the problems of greatest importance to all mankind. We cannot stand by, doing nothing, and let the world go to pieces for lack of consistency among ourselves.

We must not expect, however well we may become informed, that everything can immediately be made as it ought to be, or as it would have been if we had started the world with perfect men and women. The human condition is well expressed in the following lines, the author of which I do not know:

"Whoever thinks a faultless thing to see,
Thinks what ne'er was, nor is, nor e'er will be."

It is to the clear, plain facts that we must look. When they disclose that something is wrong, what the wrong is, and that it is plain that the wrong may be overcome, the knowledge of that condition should be so self-evident to all right-minded people that no opposition to the change from wrong to right would dare be interposed. No great, just cause can be won on personalities, nor can any individual, useful group stand isolated and win for itself, if it does not give due consideration to all the other useful groups. Temporary success or advantage, selfishly followed, will in the end yield defeat. The welfare of all must be foremost in our civic organization. When the general welfare is protected, the individual will be safe in his rights. The Preamble to the Constitution states it as it should be:

"We, the people of the United States, in order to form a more perfect union, establish justice, insure domestic tranquility, provide for the common defense, promote the general welfare, and secure the blessings of liberty to ourselves and our posterity, do ordain and establish this Constitution for the United States of America."

The Constitution has not been interpreted entirely as its founders intended it, but it still remains the Constitution, and its ultimate interpretation lies with the people themselves. The people in their wisdom, to be gained from a study of themselves and of their rights, have the power to interpret the Constitution and make it conform to the spirit of the Preamble. The Constitution provides for its own adjustment to meet the ever-changing conditions of time. All that it requires of us is knowledge of ourselves, and the power of united support of our rights.

III

THE AMERICAN FEDERATIONS

Useful organizations exist, formed by farmers, wage workers, professional workers, professional and business people, which have in whole or in part the purpose of improving industrial and business conditions, but the several organizations have no common ground for all to coordinate their work and adjust their differences.

The purposes of association are educational—to bring together the individuals in the farm, labor and useful business groups to work for just industrial and business relations, to prevent waste, to safeguard all against being exploited for selfish and improper purposes of any kind.

Associations should oppose any individual's or group of individuals', corporate or incorporate, engaged in business or industry, being guaranteed by law a "profit" or "subsidy" that must be paid by other individuals, or other groups of equal or greater importance in the world's activities, that have no guarantee; for, by reason of being forced to pay the specially privileged a subsidy or profit, those thus forced to pay are deprived of full compensation for their own service. Practices of that character have been forced upon the people by acts of public servants, clothed with legislative, executive and judicial authority. The Federal Reserve Act and the Esch-Cummins Railway Act we cite as recent examples, both of which should be materially amended or repealed, with new laws passed to protect the rights of all in this and every other regard.

Farmers, wage workers and others engaged in the necessary fields of industry and business, by reason of exorbitant taxes and the imposition of being forced to support the few especially privileged, have been reduced to bare subsistence and almost wholesale bankruptcy. It has come to a condition where the most useful occupations are paid the least, the less useful ones more, and the least useful and the useless the most. Those and other conditions, if continued, endanger the very existence of the government itself. It is again "Taxation without Representation."

Honest politics and fair business on one side have been shackled by a copartnership between unfair and dishonest business and politics on the opposite side. The means to escape is to become better informed in the true economic principles and the means to practically control business by honest political action—leaving individuals all the initiative that can be exercised without trespass upon the common welfare, and thus encouraging the highest degree of industry and thrift.

We shall become less partisan working with an organization where all our group rights are measured in a practical way, to coordinate one with another. Our rights will be defined so we may understand them, and our purposes will be fixed, so that our combined influence will become a power that cannot be flaunted or evaded by any official body. Knowing our necessities and the justice of our demands, we shall give them publicity from group to group; through the press when the press will publish; preach them from every forum where justice is favored; discuss them in our neighborhood groups; use mimeographed letters from a common headquarters, where that seems necessary; pass on from member to member; in fact, use all means necessary to spread the actual truth to support demands for justice. Knowledge should be individual as well as collective, so that the common welfare shall receive support from all of us. It is therefore simply a plan for us to help ourselves instead of stupidly remaining in a state of unrest, all the time hoping for politicians or other individuals to rescue us.

We must become independent of leadership in politics. Blindly following simply leads us to misfortune—leads us into the traps of machine rule, which has always been in the interest of the big profiteers.

IV

WORLD RELATIONS

In the first chapters of this book, the need of *justice* in rules or laws to control the relations of people with each other was considered. In the same spirit, I want to discuss international *justice* to govern the nations in their conduct towards each other. To run off into dreams of beautiful harmony between the peoples of the world would serve no good purpose, as long as the fundamental elements of discord remain. If the people of one nation cannot reasonably adjust themselves in their domestic relations, which they do not, we should not expect the nations whose peoples have strong racial prejudices to accord internationally. Justice exists only in a limited degree, either nationally or internationally. There is a lot of friction to be worked out. About the best we can do is to consider international matters in the light of circumstances, and be broad and generous enough to waive our own prejudices. We, of America, are by no means free from prejudice.

Our own affairs must be made to accord with justice before we can exercise much international influence. We must realize that the world is not benefitted by war, and drop from our consideration the power we have to form a war machine and force our influence in that way. To subdue any self-respecting people by war simply intensifies racial prejudices and makes the world worse to live in, especially when the victor is arbitrary and merciless as well as without sense.

America is not without its international faults, but in comparison with other nations, we have reason to feel proud, or at least need not feel so much regret as the other great powers should. The Civil War, a conflict between sections of our own people, is not exactly comparable with the conflicts between peoples of different nations, but is nevertheless an example to prove the wisdom of treating the vanquished whether of our own blood or foreign, with decent and respectful consideration. Our behavior in the Spanish-American War is better than history records of the other great powers in their peace terms with conquered nations. The Spaniards were required to pay no money indemnity, but on the contrary, after conquering Spain, we helped her rebuild by a contribution of $20,000,000. We went to that war to free an oppressed people, our neighbors the Cubans, and rendered no bill against Cuba. Porto Rico, which we now control, is by its location better suited to be governed by us than by Spain, even had Spain been equally liberal in dealing with the Porto Ricans. The Philippine Islands fell into our hands practically by accident, and will be freed. In the treaty for peace, after the World War, we called for neither indemnity nor territory. These facts and others prove that in our national character we are less greedy than the other great powers, and therefore are entitled to respectful hearing.

Nations will never be free from international troubles while dominated and led by politicians, or diplomats. The first consideration of those individuals is to magnify their own powers. We need not go far back for examples of failure, for during the last few years we have had all kinds of them jammed into consideration. President Wilson made great, noble proposals for the peace tribunal at Versailles. His proposals cheered the world, but the prospect of becoming President of the League of Nations left him too timid to press his projects, so they were all tabled by selfish diplomats. Lloyd George did not prove the statesman, when he was Premier of England making the Versailles Treaty, that he is now when he has been ousted from office. These two great intellects, with the power of the world behind them to influence the terms of the treaty, signed for that which they both knew was impossible of being carried out. It was generally understood by sober thinking people that the hysteria of the world at the time caused them to draft a treaty that would not be workable. But if that should be admitted we could reason that they were largely responsible for the hysteria, by not giving to the world the exact truth they knew, and which Lloyd George's later published articles proved. These men lost the opportunity of "making the world safe to live in," for which the common people supposed they fought. These great men should have known the danger of letting people, at least of their own countries, believe things without knowing. They and others in the high offices, were naturally looked to by the people for the truth, and when they failed to speak and clear up the misrepresentations of the press the people were led astray.

Adroit falsehoods have been foisted upon the people during every period, to prepare the way for selfish purposes, but 1914 to 1923 is the period of grossest misrepresentation and contradictions, with graft and wholesale and scandalous criminal profiteering never equaled in any national period at any time. Entire populations of nations — universally —had forced upon them false propaganda, and were ordered to accept without question the false as the true, and to reject the true as the false. During that period, to lie and to deceive, to speak and to write contrary to the truth was to be "patriotic." To teach hate was looked upon as a virtue. Men and women, and even children, were forced to deny themselves the opportunity of listening to, and much less learning, the truth in matters of the most vital importance. The constituted authorities, in numerous cases, encouraged mobs to keep the truth from being told. The suppression of truth was a cover to gigantic graft and profiteering schemes which were carried out even with the help of public officials. If by accident honest persons discovered the truth, they had to deny and instead support the propaganda of the nations' betrayers. The different peoples of the earth were forced to shut their eyes and close their ears to the truth and stop thinking, and by no possible chance could they resort to reason, for it was ordained by the dynasties, including our own high officials, that the world conflicts should hold the reasoning powers in a state of aberation, at the same time forcing people to make all kinds of sacrifices, even to mortgaging their futures and the future of their children. So strongly entrenched were the profiteers that even honest, intelligent people who knew the falsehood of it all were afraid to speak. In the face of that condition the Treaty of Versailles was made, and the world now faces bedlam—a world's madhouse looms before us—unless the plain people shall act to redeem it.

Think of it—a group of nations joined, as they claimed, to destroy the mightiest war machine the world had known—the German—proclaiming that it menaced the love and peace of the world. The Allies made the sacrifice to destroy that war machine. That it was a terrible sacrifice all admit. What a travesty, after doing so for the love and peace of the world, that the terms of peace should have been left to the "GRAND OLD MEN" who never sacrificed, but made the Treaty of Versailles impossible of fulfillment by the vanquished. To complete the travesty two of the Allies, for which the principal sacrifice had been made, reared up out of their own dust and shell-shattered soil a still greater war machine to challenge "the love and peace of the world" and invade the country that the Versailles Treaty stripped of the opportunity of self-defense. That new war machine rapes a defenseless nation. Of course, always in war, each side will lie about the other, to make it appear that the other is to blame. Ordinarily we cannot affirm or deny the statements, for we do not usually have the proof. One thing we do know, however, and that is that Germany has no army to defend itself against the war machine of France and Belgium, and another fact is known: and that is, that France and Belgium have invaded Germany. That is the greatest possible offense and breach of trust against their former allies.

Is there an example in history where the sacrifices of the peoples of nations have been so quickly and shamelessly violated? The world had been bled white to make it "a better place to live in," and the politicians of France and Belgium (whose people were saved by the other Allies' sacrifice, God save their people, for they are led and act on orders) have violated every semblance of human judgment in needlessly challenging again the peace of the world. Civilization has already paid the penalty for its system of false economic dealing. Can we trust nations? Answer is unnecessary, for history responds with sickening certainty.

In the World War, the peoples of the nations fought for entirely different purposes than were the purposes of the public officials and profiteers who directed the course of things. If anyone won, it was the profiteers. The catastrophe has been so great, however, that even they now question whether they did not make a mistake. America is realizing the mistake, and because of that realization may not be camouflaged again into a useless struggle.

When we look the truth in the face, we are forced to admit that the peoples of the earth have tripped upon the civilization of their own creation. They see that it is faulty—so faulty that it threatens the destruction of humanity unless a better plan is developed. The reasons for its failures were explained in a former chapter. Great statesmanship may develop in the people of one country, but unless it also springs up in the other countries the world as a whole will not be safe. It is possible, however, for a country as great as our own, the United States, to build its own civilization without encountering obstructive interference from other countries, and if the other nations continue to act as unwisely as most of them give evidence, it is our duty to keep independent of much dealing with them. Because of our power in population, our geographical size and advantage in position and material resources, we can be absolutely independent within ourselves, and have little if any reliance on the rest of the world for anything. While we do not desire to isolate ourselves, even that would be preferable to the conditions that exist across the waters. If we took the position of independence, we could easily pull ourselves out of our present inexcusable economic absurdity, and at the same time exercise a moral influence over the rest of the world that would in time show the means for world redemption. It is self-evident that we cannot redeem the world by war. It is also evident that unless we lead in something better, either some other country will have to show the way, or humanity will fail entirely.

Let us look to a few facts of our own. We have every material resource necessary to make us independent. Our people have the intelligence, the industry and the mechanical devices to produce more than we can use or consume; we have the transportation systems to carry the products from place of production to place of consumption. Nothing is lacking in physical conditions, and still want and poverty stalk over our country and make us almost as absurd as the warring countries across the waters.

A cloud hangs over America's big profiteers. They have gathered in the bulk of the world's gold, and stored it in the vaults of their great banks. The spectre of world demonetization of gold, or what would amount to that, appears before them to destroy their bulwark. More war brings that spectre nearer. Our whole nation is governed by the almighty dollar, the most dishonest dollar that civilization, with all the financial geniuses of the world, has been able to invent. In the last three years it has robbed the American farmer of approximately $20,000,000,000 and wage workers and small business of other colossal sums. A few big bankers dominate the dollar and it absolutely dominates our industries, and with it the credit of the people is appropriated for the benefit of those big bankers. Let it not be thought however that to create an honest dollar will get us out of trouble, for the dishonest dollar has already unbalanced the economic conditions, and in large measure the mental attitude of the people is not ready for them to be advantaged simply creating honest money. Our whole economic system requires to be treated with common sense. We must remove our prejudices and do straight thinking, instead of taking the thoughts that the profiteers feed us through the press and otherwise. If we make use of our opportunities, and put our house in condition, the rest of the world will quickly follow. We must at once, if we do our duty, create an honest dollar. A dollar that the Federal Reserve bank alone controls cannot be honest. The other legislation to correct the unbalanced economic conditions will quickly follow and our country will be put in a permanently prosperous condition. The rest of the world will see it and follow the example.

Are we, the United States, likely to lead? That is doubtful, for we have not been tried to the limit by poverty and disease, and many are scared to leave the old wreck while any part of it can be used. There is a new world psychology taking shape. Humanity is becoming ashamed of the civil—rather uncivil—relations that exist between humans. It sees the farce of the past and present. The masses realize that they have the power, and that instead of their using it for themselves, their oppressors have used the power of the masses to make the world a poor place for the masses to live in. If we think that the same practices that brought on the world chaos may be continued for the purpose of getting out of chaos, we are going to be very much fooled. We shall have to have in the future a very different system of dealing with problems than we have had in the past.

Many are asking themselves what is to come out of this world confusion. Certainly we are not so cowardly as to give up. Not we, at least, stepping aside as Americans, for we have not exhausted our opportunities in the United States. We have simply failed to make the most reasonable use of them. If as a people we stop to think and consider what we have been doing, we shall find that we have been following leaders and doing little if any thinking for ourselves, a lazy and ridiculous failure on our part. Take for example our entry into the World War. We did not think. We elected a president for a second term because he said he "kept us out of war" in his first term. We proved by a large vote that we did not want to go to war, but no sooner was the president re-elected, than the propaganda started to put us in the war. Then we became hysterical, as people always have done in war, and we believed everything bad against our enemy and believed only good of our allies and ourselves. As a matter of fact all the leaders were bad, vicious.

They lost their reason and the people followed. We accused the Germans of having created a war machine to dominate the world, and yet the Germans were surrounded on all sides by enemies with more war machines. Each was afraid of the other. These war machines were created to do the very things that they afterwards did. We cannot properly blame the people of any of the European nations, unless we blame ourselves still more. None of them were free from danger of the others, and did not dare to trust each other lest their trust should be betrayed. We, however, were not in danger, statements by the profiteers and militarists to the contrary notwithstanding. We were far removed from the firebrands—a mighty nation in potential power, which could defend itself. Did we expect the winner, whichever it might be, to come over here for more war? None who could understand the effects of that war had any such notion. The greatest good we could do the world at that time was to stay out, and that would have been infinitely better for ourselves, for we could have helped the world had we conserved our resources. There never was a nation that did a more unstatesmanlike thing than we did to enter the war. We came out without establishing a single principle for which we entered, and it was as plain as "A, B, C" before we started, just what we would get out of it. Some of us may still be prejudiced about the war, but those who are can have never taken an inventory of the circumstances. About 98 per cent of the people of our country have been severely punished for our part in the engagement and since the world is not better, but is worse, with no prospect for betterment in sight, the one great compelling duty of America is to put its own house in shape, and to stand upon an economic system that will make its natural resources available to the intelligence, industry and use of the people. When we do that the way to world redemption from the folly of present chaos will stand out in our country so clearly, honestly and usefully that we shall be copied wherever peoples do their own thinking.

V

"BY THE PEOPLE—FOR THE PEOPLE"

We shall never be able to protect our rights by mere surface observations. We have to deal with fundamental problems. We have been led astray by catch words and phrases used as an appeal to sentiment, when back of it all were conditions governed by men forming inner circles, acting in secret against the common interest. We have had no way of securing information on matters of the greatest importance to us in our everyday affairs. We are continually being taken by surprise—meeting losses that we could have avoided by any reasonable system of keeping informed.

The larger business interests have their checking-up agencies, and are not often so taken by surprise as to be losers. R. G. Dunn & Co., the Bradstreet Agency, Babson's Agency and others make a specialty of keeping track of everything that influences business present and business prospective, even to the detailed affairs of individuals, and are at all times prepared to give valuable information to their clients. All of them are available and used by the big business houses. Their reports not only touch on finance, but deal with everything the world over that affects business. While some of these agencies make press statements it is only the mere surface matters that they make public. Their most valuable information is not available, or at least not easy for the people to secure, because of the expense for one thing, and because much of their information is personal in its character and therefore confidential.

We plain people rely mostly upon the press for our information. The last eight years form an example of how badly it works. The press furnished no advance index of business conditions. The press forecasts were always too late or entirely misleading. The agencies whose special business it was and is to furnish reports did furnish the information that saved many of their clients from bankruptcy.

We who had no advisory agency were taken into the inflation and deflation periods with no notice except as the events themselves were brought upon us. During the period from 1914 to now, April, 1923, the press has failed utterly to serve the people with valuable advice about either inflation or deflation. As a fact, it misled us and, what is worse, it did so designedly in many instances. The then current events made it very clear that certain radically changing conditions would result as a matter of course, but the press gave no warning. The few of us who understood what was bound to follow had no way of giving the information to the masses.

Inflation and deflation were a matter of financing, engineered by less than a dozen men well known to the metropolitan press. That those men would control in the interest of the profiteers was as certain as the daily rising and setting of the sun. Should any one of those few or all of them have died, the law is such that they would have been succeeded by the same kind, and all things would have been just the same. It is not a criticism of the men who control so much as of the system to which these men fall heir. By their arbitrary acts we were led along, helping ourselves, to run up prices until unwittingly we believed that they would always last. Then that same little group arbitrarily reversed its action and directed the period of deflation. Of both acts the big profiteers had advance notice. In fact, they were in the scheme, for they were ready to scalp from the unsuspecting people many billions of profit by deflation, as they had already by inflation. The plain workers and the most useful industrial and smaller business groups were in ignorance of both plans till they were caught by deflation and many bankrupted. It is a scheme of the big profiteers to carry out the system that rules. As long as things are done that way times will move in cycles of ups and downs. While that condition lasts, a good crop and healthy stock will not insure success to the farmer, nor will honest effort on the part of the wage worker be a guarantee of success to him; and as the useful business groups are dependent on the farmer and the wage worker, the consequence to the useful business interests will be the same.

There are no politicians and there are no political parties that will get us out of trouble until first we know what our troubles are, and how to remedy them. Public officials in sufficient numbers will not serve us until we know how they can do it and tell them, backing our demand with strong sentiment expressed. Politicians are cowards and never knowingly face opposition when it looks formidable.

The whole world is in trouble over industrial and living conditions. The different peoples find the forms and practices of political action, to remedy known wrongs, either entirely blocked, or so slow and doubtful in operation that many foreign peoples have come to believe in direct action to avoid the uncertainty and delay of remedy through the constituted governments, especially when their governments are controlled by oppressors. We people of Columbia must beware of that condition and act by our constitutional rights before too many of us lose faith in our political institutions. If we were to overthrow our government by violence we would still have trouble—more trouble than we have now.

The Russian people, with ample excuse because of a lack of voice in the old monarchy, took direct, successful action. It was the only thing they could do if they were to become free. Ireland too, not so lacking as the Russians in a voice of the people's wishes, was nevertheless weak in having its will put into execution, and took direct action. Germany, Austria, Italy, Turkey, Hungary, Portugal, Greece, Mexico, and others have had the fist of the people against the face of existing government.

We have had no mass demonstration against our government, but there are organizations continually preying upon the people, whom the authorities hunt down. Faster than they are put down others are formed, apparently, and it does not seem possible to stop these acts against the laws under existing circumstances. Simultaneously the big interest groups too exploit the people, and they are supported by the authorities that be.

The laws have become very much distrusted by the plain people in nearly all countries and justice is looked upon as impotent under present conditions. Politics have failed to bring relief. In fact, politics have been manipulated against the peoples. Even in our own country it is very certain that if we wish to remain a great nation some fundamental, constructive work must take place before the masses lose respect for all constituted government.

We find ourselves compelled to take notice of the serious conditions. By proper constitutional action we must overcome the difficulties described in previous pages. If we do not the direct-action contagion of Europe and all the Orient will threaten us too, and that soon.

There is nothing lacking in our country for the people to control when once we properly inform ourselves. Political machinery for control is provided in the Constitution itself, and there are some laws, too, that we can use to put things in proper order. But a knowledge of things as they are and the means necessary to overcome wrongs and maintain rights is required. Many organizations are doing great work for correction, but there is none that covers the entire field of industrial and business relations of all the different useful groups to combining them into a solid force.

The facts presented in Books I and II relate mainly to industrial, commercial and physical conditions, and the relations that politics hold to them. It is an appeal to the mind—to reason—for thought on material things. If we are compelled to bedraggle ourselves through most of our wakeful hours to minister merely to our physical wants, life in its higher purposes becomes dwarfed. If we look upon ourselves merely as a state or nation, as a concrete whole, —the way those in power seek to have us—and forget ourselves as individuals, we and the state and the nation all become failures. Nations exist fundamentally for the peoples—not the peoples for the nations. Because of nations acting as governments independent of the people, dominating the people and conscripting the people and the products of their toil, Europe and all the Orient is in a most dangerous condition. We of America are not without our internal danger.

We can banish from our minds the thought that the people live for the nation, because the nation is for the people and it must be preserved for the people of the present and future. In no other way can it have full strength. It is treason to sacrifice the people for the government, except when it is necessary to have the nation for the people present and future. By the power of the nation's support, the life and expression of the people must be maintained. The nation is not national for purposes of death, but is national for the purposes of the life of the national human family—which ultimately will include the people of all the world, guided by the spirit of justice everywhere. That will be the least costly and the most effective, but the world is not yet fit for such a condition. Too much racial prejudice exists. It would not work.

Partisanship without relation to the higher purposes has destroyed the strength of the individual. That accounts for our being hero worshipers, flocking to see and hear this or that noted person whom we have heard about. Too often we go as worshipers instead of reasoners. When we go in that way we belittle ourselves. Unless the hero of our mind happens to be really great and good enough to lead us to our own individuality and make us feel our own importance as thinking beings, thinking out all things for ourselves, our mind hero has served no good purpose, nor have we been strengthened. Unless we acquire strength by our own independence of thought, we simply go on blocking the way for those who are right and have the strength.

Truth must be our authority for everything. There is no other authority. Truth must be reached through the individual mind and not through the arbitrary acceptance of the words of imagined heroes who have not the facts to reinforce their statements. We must welcome the fellowship of men and women in order to make life the most useful force in the world. The one great person must be the individual, for himself—to make himself consistent with the rights of every other to be as high and as important as is he. In no other way can we have the full strength of the nation. In no other way can the masses get their rights. We must substitute reason for tradition—if we are ever to unshackle ourselves from the arbitrary domination of property privilege over human right.

THE END

GENERAL INDEX

Bank deposits: mostly credit, not money, 80, 81.
Banks, 1892 challenge of big, 62.
Banks, Federal Reserve, *see* "Banks and the People," 77-83.
Banks, Federal Reserve, as spies on people, 91, 92.
Banks, strong and weak, defined, 77, 78, 79.

Capital: its strikes called hard times, 32.
Capital's fortresses: unearned profit, 37, 38.
Chambers of Commerce: United States, International, 18, 74.
Congress, contributions of, to trusts, 72, 73, 84, 89, 90, 106, 107, 113.
Congressmen, empty promises of, 36.

Dollars: honest and dishonest, 231.

Education, college and other, 166.
Exports: when justified, 173, 174, 175.

Farmer and wage worker, no guarantee to, 33.
Farmer deceived, 29, 70, 89, 111, 112, 114, 119, 191, 192, 205.

Farmer, wage worker, small business man, hard luck of, 10, 11, 12.

Franco-Belgian invasion of Germany, 228.

Gold, grabbing of, 86, 88, 98, 101, 118.

Government and nation, the difference between, 182, 183.

Government in partnership with robbers, 172, 173.

Groups: useful and useless, 17, 18, 19.

Inflation and deflation, 93.

Inner circles, 136.

Labor and property, status of, 26, 40, 47, 48, 49, 50, 53.

Labor products greater than any other wealth, 21-5.

Labor, purpose of capital to subordinate, right or wrong, 125, 126.

Liberty bonds: first buying enforced, then selling, 31, 106.

Life, lower order of, 156, 158.

Mortgage on our backs, 107, 108.

Panics, 94, 95.

People helpless until further legislation, 88.

People without definite plans, 14, 15.

Price fixers, 22, 161, 162.

Producers and consumers: how kept apart, 104, 105.

Profits outlaw Constitution, 52.

Progressives, 15, 171, 175, 177, 179, 206, 209, 233.

Railroad Labor Board: findings inconsistent, 33.

Railroads: employment of "scabs" while public pays the bill, 123, 124.

Reason, need for, 110, 111.
Repudiation, 110, 111.

Senator, U. S., defies Labor, 57, 58.
Strikes forced by law, alternative slavery, 58.

Trusts: agreement among themselves and with politicians, 122.

Unshackling, 244, 245.

Voters, responsibility of, 178, 182, 183, 237.

Wage worker, no guarantee to, 33.
Wages, farm products, minimum price for, 38.
War prices, 99.
Wealth: a liability or asset, 27, 28.
Winners, the, 202, 203.
Workers, province of, 184, 185, 186.
World War: our entry a mistake 233, 234.